The Complete
OUTDOOR GAS GRIDDLE
Cookbook

Easy & Hassle-Free Recipes for Breakfast, Burgers, Meat, Vegetables and Other Delicious Meals to Have Memorable Outdoor Parties

Pitmaster Academy

© Copyright 2022 by Pitmaster Academy - All rights reserved.

The content contained within this book may not be reproduced, duplicated, or transmitted without direct written permission from the author or the publisher. Under no circumstances will any blame or legal responsibility be held against the publisher, or author, for any damages, reparation, or monetary loss due to the information contained within this book. Either directly or indirectly.

Legal Notice: This book is copyright protected. This book is only for personal use. You cannot amend, distribute, sell, use, quote, or paraphrase any part, or the content within this book, without the consent of the author or publisher.

Disclaimer Notice: Please note the information contained within this document is for educational and entertainment purposes only. All effort has been executed to present accurate, up-to-date, reliable, and complete information. No warranties of any kind are declared or implied. Readers acknowledge that the author is not engaged in rendering legal, financial, medical, or professional advice. The content within this book has been derived from various sources. Please consult a licensed professional before attempting any techniques outlined in this book.

By reading this document, the reader agrees that under no circumstances is the author responsible for any losses, direct or indirect, incurred as a result of the use of the information contained within this document, including, but not limited to, errors, omissions, or inaccuracies.

TABLE OF CONTENTS

06 INTRODUCTION

11 BREAKFAST

18 BURGERS

28 RUBS

39 PORK

53 BEEF

65 POULTRY

81 LAMB

93 SEAFOOD

103 VEGETABLE

114 CONCLUSION

115 APPENDIX:
A - CONVERSION CHART
B - RECIPE INDEX

INTRODUCTION

Outdoor gas griddles have long been used as cookware widely in restaurants and diners to offer us mesmerizing hot staples and dishes. The Griddle is one of the most affordable cooking appliances you can buy, and it has a long-life span. Using a gas griddle to cook is safer, easier, and faster than using a kitchen stove. As a home cook always on the road, I have been using outdoor gas griddles for years. The traditional range of features and cooking options you get with an outdoor gas griddle will impress you with its portability and ease of use.

An outdoor gas griddle is an outstanding appliance that cooks large volumes of food in a small area with less effort. With this appliance, you can enjoy excellent quality meals and save money. An outdoor gas griddle is a must-have if you frequently prepare meals for guests or find yourself cooking for large families on many occasions. It is also great for caterers and restaurants that must cook lots of food simultaneously. The gas griddle is also very helpful in camping and back-country cooking.

If you have tiny kitchen space, don't want to clean the kitchen floor, have never used the oven before, or need a fast and easy way to cook for people who drop by unexpectedly, an outdoor gas griddle is what you should use. It will take minutes to heat up and cook your favorite foods on a gas griddle. The outdoor gas griddle is a one-stop solution for all your cooking needs in and out of your kitchen.

The book will teach you everything you need to know about using a gas grill outside. Before using this appliance, I will go through the basic steps that you need to know. This book will also go through some common mistakes made by first-time users that I have seen in the past.

This cookbook will show you the best ways and techniques to grill, but it will also provide you with many beneficial tips and an extensive array of sumptuous grilled recipes that you can only find in this cookbook. I will also talk in this cookbook about the best cooking techniques to control the temperature; with the help of a griddle, maintain your grill flat, and don't give up on a large array of sumptuous recipes you will never regret tasting.

Benefits of Gas Griddle

Outdoor gas griddle cooking offers many benefits. Let's see all these benefits one by one.

1. Large and Flat Surface Cooking

One of the main benefits of the gas griddle is its large and flat cooking surface. Compared to a frying pan, the big cooking area allows you to cook more food items at once, and flipping food is simple. On the Griddle, you can cook a lot of things. The large cooking surface doesn't retain moisture and gives you a crispy cooking result. It's an excellent choice for larger families who want to consume eggs, bacon, hotdogs, burgers, and vegetables at backyard gatherings.

2. Excellent Built Quality

The gas grills are made up of high-quality stainless steel materials.
The primary cooking surface is made up of rolled, high-quality 7-gauge steel.
The entire body surface is covered with a black powder coating which protects it from rust.

3. Runs on Propane Gas

The gas grills use propane gas for cooking your food. Compared to charcoal fuel, propane gas never creates smoke and harmful gases while cooking food in your backyard. Propane griddles are easy to start all you just need to do is turn the dial, and the burner fired up. The gas griddle can maintain a steady temperature, and your Griddle takes less than 15 minutes to reach its maximum temperature.

4. Versatile

The gas griddle is one of the versatile outdoor cooking appliances that offer to cook most of the foods over a smooth cooking surface. The gas griddle is equipped with four burners which allow you to operate them individually. The Griddle can cook different types of food at different temperatures simultaneously. You can make pancakes, eggs, waffles, steak, burgers, hot dogs, and more with perfection on the gas griddle.

5. Easy to Clean

Clean the Griddle is one of the easy tasks. You just need to clean the greasy cooking area. You can use a spatula or Griddle to scrap up grease to clean grease. Use a paper towel to wipe the cooking surface, and finally, give the touch-up with a scouring pad.

How To Do Before the First Use

It's easy to let those recipes start pouring through your thoughts and start preparing for that first wonderful meal when you first get the griddle home and rip open the package.

However, there are a few things you need to do before you start cooking to ensure that you don't break your new Griddle and that everything goes as planned.

1. Wash your Griddle

This may sound beyond obvious. Many people tend to skip this step.

When your brand-new Griddle comes out of its box, it will be covered in protective grease and oil. This isn't the type of grease you want on the surface of your grill, as it can smoke up your food.

Instead, please wash it with hot soapy water before cooking anything, and after each time you use it.

2. Select a Cooking Oil

The kind of oil you use on your Griddle will significantly affect its performance. When choosing a cooking oil for use on a griddle, look for one with a high smoke point. You'll also want some oil that will assist you in generating the smooth layered covering that keeps your Griddle from sticking. There are many different types of oils, but the most popular for

Griddle are Grape Seed Oil, Avocado Oil, Olive Oil, and Flaxseed Oil.

3. **Season Your Griddle**

This is a crucial stage that should not be overlooked. I suppose it could, but it would spoil your cooking experience and leave you wondering why people are so fond of griddles. Between the naked skillet iron and the food you're cooking, the seasoning process generates a hardened barrier. Your seasoning transforms into a bullet-proof, non-stick surface barrier that outperforms most store-bought "non-stick" pans. Your Griddle will never lose its non-stick ability if you use it properly and season it

How To Maintain and Clean

The proper storage and maintenance are necessary to increase the lifespan of your Griddle. The following steps guide you in the storage and maintenance of your Griddle.

- **After Each Use, Clean Your Griddle**

When you start using your Griddle, it seasons automatically after each use. Cleaning is one of the essential steps to keep your Griddle clean and hygienic. Clean the griddle surface with hot water and a paper towel. Do not use soapy water to clean the cooking surface; instead, use a scrapper. Clean and dry paper towels can wipe down the greasy feeling.

- **Remove Rust**

If you find any rust spots over the Griddle, then use 40 or 60 low grit sandpaper, or you can also use steel wool to remove the rust spot and scrub them properly.

- **Coat Griddle After Cleaning**

After finishing the cleaning process apply a thin coat of cooking spray over the griddle cooking surface to prevent rusting built up the overcooking surface area of the Griddle.

- **Store And Maintain Griddle**

After finishing all the cleaning steps store your Griddle in a cool and dry place. To prevent dust, always keep your Griddle covered and keep it away from the humid area.

Tips on How Best to Use the Outdoor Gas Griddle

Here are some top tips to remember to have the best experience when using your outdoor gas griddle.

- **Open the Propane Tank Slowly**

As a best practice, open the propane tank valve slowly. Opening the valve too fast can make the regulator faulty, resulting in low or uneven flames. Taking it slowly each time will help avoid regulator issues and the desired blue solid flame. If the problem keeps coming up, you might want to disconnect the regulator from the tank and reconnect it again. It might be necessary to replace the regulator if the problem persists.

- **Increase Temperature Slowly**

When you start cooking, set the burners to a low temperature. Increasing the temperature of the Griddle slowly is better than doing so quickly. If it is done too fast, you run the risk of warping the metal surface so that it is no longer flat. If you put something frozen on a boiling cooking surface, this might also happen. So, start low and let it heat up before raising the temperature.

- **Disposable Drip Pans**

All outdoor griddles have a grease trap because of the excess food and grease cooking on a griddle. You can make the disposal of this mess quick and easy by using a foil drip pan, and cleaning up would be as simple as throwing the drip pan in the trash instead of cleaning the mess out of the metal trap.

- **Use Spray Oil**

You will regularly be applying cooking oil to the cooking surface when using your outdoor Griddle. Squirt bottles are great, but a quicker and easier way to apply oil is to use oil in a spray bottle. Spray bottles allow you to easily apply a thin coat of oil to the Griddle without having to clean out a bottle later. The squirt bottles can still be helpful for water or sauces.

- **Use Water**

Water can be the most beneficial element when using your outdoor gas griddle. It can be used for loosening hard residual food, cleaning any other residue, and you can steam vegetables.

When using a scrapper, add some water to the affected area and allow the steam to help loosen the stuck-on food. Once you have cleared all the food, there might be some black or brown residue remaining on your Griddle, and it will come off easily using some water and paper towels.

And all you need to do to steam some vegetables is place them on the cooking surface, spray some water on them, and use a basting cover. The heat should evaporate the water, and the basting cover should keep it trapped, steaming your food.

- **Prepare Everything Ahead of Time**

Another best practice is to have everything ready before you start cooking. The great thing about a gas griddle is that it can cook things quickly, but it does not leave you time to run inside for something or prepare anything while the food is cooking. Before you put anything onto the Griddle, make sure that you have everything you will need within arm's reach. This includes all your tools and the food you will be cooking on the Griddle. You can prep, slice, season, or measure food ahead of time so that you only have to prepare it at the last minute.

Use Wax or Parchment Paper Between Uses

For added protection against rust and bugs or other small animals, cover your Griddle's cooking surface with wax or parchment paper. Follow your normal cleaning process and allow the Griddle to cool completely before placing a sheet of wax or parchment paper on the cooking surface.

- **Cook at Low or Medium Temperature**

Many individuals cook at higher temperatures, which can degrade the quality of their food and cause more food to stick to the Griddle. Most foods should be cooked at a temperature of 300 to 350 degrees Fahrenheit; however, some things benefit from higher temperatures. However, you'll want to cook on low or medium heat most of the time. For example, you should increase the heat when searing a steak, but eggs or pancakes should be cooked at a lower temperature. You should set the temperature according to what you're cooking, so bear that in mind.

- **Cover Your Griddle**

Maintaining your outdoor gas griddle is essential and avoiding moisture is your biggest concern. Hardcovers and softcovers are highly recommended for protecting your Griddle from the elements. You can prevent this by placing something between the cooking surface or hardcover and the softcover to elevate it so that any water will run down the sides instead of pooling at the top. If you keep your outdoor, You don't have to worry about this if you keep the Griddle under a covered location between uses. This is a beautiful suggestion for protecting your Griddle if it is exposed to the outdoors.

How to Smoke with your Griddle

Do you want to know if you can smoke on a griddle? You're probably hoping to get that excellent smokey flavor in your cuisine without having to invest in a dedicated smoker or spending a lot of money.

Don't worry; we won't advise you to spend all of your money. We've devised a simple method for using your flat top grill as a smoker.

1. First and foremost, you must construct the smoker box, which will require two aluminum foil pans. The base will be the first aluminum foil pan, and the lid will be the second. These pans may be found in most online stores. You should be aware, however, that the weight capacity of each pan varies. As a result, make sure you purchase a 19X11X4-inch spatial pan. You'll also require racks, aluminum foil, and a meat thermometer. Choose a rack that is slightly smaller (but not too small) than the pan and ensure that it fits snugly inside the pan.

2. After you've gathered all of these goods, keep one rack and cover the surface with aluminum foil. This is where the drip tray will be.

3. It's time to start building the smoker box. Cut the bottom side of the aluminum pan. Keep in mind that this stage is a little challenging. To put the legs of the rack into the pan, trim the bottom half of the pan but leave at 2 cm to 3 cm on each side. Place the drip tray we built earlier inside the pan once you've finished this step.

4. Cut aluminum foil into a rectangle form with a knife. We'll create another tray to store sawdust in. Fold the aluminum foil one cm from each side at least two to three times after cutting it.

5. Only one more step remains, which is to construct a homemade temperature gauge. You'll need a meat thermometer for this. So grab it and secure it to the second aluminum pan, which will serve as the smoker box's cover.

6. Put everything on the Griddle. Take the aluminum foil tray, cover it with sawdust, and place it on the Griddle. Then, holding the smokebox, insert the second rack, which we haven't used yet. This second rack will serve as our cooking surface, where the meat will be smoked. Hold the smoker box lid and place it on the smoker box after you've placed the meat. When you're ready, set this smoker box on the tray we built for the stardust.

SPINACH AND EGG SCRAMBLE

Preparation Time:
5 minutes

Cooking time:
10 minutes

Servings:
1

INGREDIENTS:

- 1/2 cup of spinach, chopped
- 3 eggs, lightly beaten
- Salt and pepper to taste
- 4 mushrooms, chopped
- 1/4 cup of bell peppers, chopped

DIRECTIONS

1. Preheat the Griddle at medium-high temperature.
2. Coat the top of the Griddle using cooking spray.
3. Place chopped vegetables on top of a hot griddle and cook till softened.
4. Stir in the eggs, pepper, & salt till the eggs are scrambled and set.
5. Enjoy your servings.

NUTRITION:

Calories 335, Fat 27g, Protein 19g, Carbs 6g

GRIDDLE PANCAKE

 Preparation Time: 10 minutes

 Cooking time: 15 minutes

 Servings: 10

INGREDIENTS:

- 4 Cups Flour
- 3 Cup Milk
- 1/2 Cup Vinegar
- 2 teaspoon Salt
- 1 tablespoon Baking Powder
- 1/2 Cup Sugar
- 2 teaspoon Baking Soda
- 1 teaspoon Baking Powdering
- 4 Eggs
- Vegetable Oil
- 1/2 Cup Butter (Melted)

DIRECTIONS

1. Combine the milk and vinegar in a bowl or dish. Allow for a 5 minutes sour period after combining the ingredients.
2. Combine the eggs and melted butter in a mixing dish or mixer.
3. While it was mixing, add the remaining ingredients in this order: salt, baking soda, baking powder, and white sugar.
4. Stir the milk mixture with a fork before pouring it into the pancake batter.
5. Allow to mix for 1 minute and then start to add your flour.
6. Preheat your griddle to medium-high heat.
7. Once your griddle is hot enough, start dispensing your pancake batter onto the griddle.
8. When your pancakes have bubbles and you can tell they're ready to flip, use a long spatula to flip them over.
9. Remove the pancakes from the pan when they are done.
10. Serve and enjoy!

NUTRITION: Calories 225, Fat 10, Protein 6g, Carbs 30g

FRENCH TOAST STICKS

Preparation Time: 10 minutes

Cooking time: 10 minutes

Servings: 2

INGREDIENTS:

- 2/3 cup of milk
- 2 eggs
- 1 teaspoon of vanilla
- 4 bread slices, cut each bread slice into 3 pieces vertically
- 1/4 teaspoon of ground cinnamon

DIRECTIONS:

1. Preheat your Griddle to a low temperature.
2. Whisk together the eggs, cinnamon, vanilla, & milk in a mixing dish.
3. Coat the top of the Griddle using cooking spray.
4. Dip each slice of bread into the egg mixture & coat thoroughly.
5. Place the coated bread pieces on the hot griddle top & cook till both sides are golden brown.
6. Enjoy your meal.

NUTRITION: Calories 166, Fat 7g, Protein 10g, Carbs 14g

SIMPLE CHEESE SANDWICH

Preparation Time:
10 minutes

Cooking time:
10 minutes

Servings:
1

INGREDIENTS:

- 2 teaspoons of butter
- 2 bread slices
- 2 cheese slices

DIRECTIONS

1. Preheat your Griddle to a low temperature.
2. Arrange cheese slices on top of one slice of bread and cover with another slice of bread.
3. Both bread pieces should be slathered in butter.
4. Cook the sandwich on a hot griddle till golden brown and the cheese has melted.
5. Enjoy your meal.

NUTRITION: Calories 340, Fat 26g, Protein 15g, Carbs 10g

TOMATO SCRAMBLED EGG

 Preparation Time: 5 minutes

 Cooking time: 10 minutes

 Servings: 2

INGREDIENTS:

- 1 tablespoon of olive oil
- 2 eggs, lightly beaten
- Salt and pepper to taste
- 2 tablespoons of fresh basil, chopped
- 1/2 tomato, chopped

DIRECTIONS:

1. Preheat your Griddle at medium-high temperature.
2. Apply oil to the Griddle's surface.
3. Cook till the tomatoes have softened.
4. Combine together the eggs, basil, pepper, & salt.
5. Cook till the eggs are set on top of the tomatoes by pouring the egg mixture over them.
6. Enjoy your meal.

NUTRITION: Calories 125, Fat 12g, Protein 6g, Carbs 1g

PEANUT BUTTER AND VANILLA TOAST

Preparation Time:
10 minutes

Cooking time:
10 minutes

Servings:
3

INGREDIENTS:

- 2 tablespoons of creamy peanut butter
- 1 cup of brown sugar
- 1 loaf of toast bread
- 1 teaspoon of grape jelly
- 1 tablespoon butter
- 1 teaspoon of vanilla extract
- ¾ cup of half and half

DIRECTIONS:

1. Make a typical PB&J sandwich with the desired jelly-to-peanut-butter ratio.
2. Combine two eggs, 1 teaspoon of vanilla, 1 cup of brown sugar, and 3/4 cup of half & half in a medium-sized mixing dish.
3. On the Griddle, melt 1 tablespoon of butter (medium-high temperature, 350°F, direct cooking).
4. Cook for around 3-5 min on the Griddle after dipping and coating the PB&J in the mixture.
5. Cook for another 3-5 min on the other side.
6. Serve while it's still hot.

NUTRITION: Calories 390, Fat 14g, Protein 11g, Carbs 29g

BURGERS

CHEESESTEAK

Preparation Time:
5 minutes

Cooking time:
10 minutes

Servings:
6

INGREDIENTS:

- (3 pounds ribeye (thinly sliced)
- buns
- 1 tbsp oil
- cheese
- butter
- peppers and onions (optional)

DIRECTIONS:

1. Preheat your gas griddle over medium heat.
2. Butter your buns and toast them quickly.
3. Put some butter on one half of the griddle, along with the onions and peppers (if you want it), and some oil on the other half. Allow it to warm, but not to the point of smoking, before adding the beef.
4. Season the beef with salt and pepper, and move it around continuously with spatulas.
5. Sprinkle cheese on top, cover with a dome, and turn the griddle off. The cheese will be melted by the residual heat.
6. Stuff your buns full of cheese-covered ribeye, add any peppers and onions you desire, and enjoy it!

NUTRITION: Calories 750, Fat 50g, Protein 60g, Carbs 5g

BEST-EVER CHEDDAR BURGERS

Preparation Time:
10 minutes

Cooking time:
10 minutes

Servings:
4

INGREDIENTS:

- 1/3 cup of fresh parsley, chopped
- 1 to 1-1/2 lbs. of ground turkey
- 1/4 cup of whole-berry cranberry sauce
- 4 buns, split and toasted
- 4 green onions, finely chopped
- 1 teaspoon of poultry seasoning
- 1 tablespoon of grill seasoning
- 1 green apple, cored and sliced thinly
- 8 leaves of green leaf lettuce
- 2 tablespoons of oil
- 8 slices of Cheddar cheese
- 2 tablespoons of spicy brown mustard

DIRECTIONS:

1. Preheat the Griddle at medium-high temperature and brush a thin layer of olive oil on it.
2. Form 4 patties from the turkey, parsley, onions, and seasonings. In a heated griddle. The patties should take around 5 minutes on each side if you want the center to not be pink.
3. Remove the patties and cover to allow the cheese to melt. Combine the cranberry sauce & mustard and spread it on the cut sides of the buns.
4. Close sandwiches by adding lettuce and burgers.

NUTRITION: Calories 534, Fat 29g, Protein 36g, Carbs 29g

ITALIAN HAMBURGERS

Preparation Time:
10 minutes

Cooking time:
20 minutes

Servings:
6

INGREDIENTS:

- 1 1/2 lbs. of ground beef
- 1/2 cup of Italian-flavored dry breadcrumbs
- 6 hamburger buns, split
- 2 eggs, beaten
- 2 slices of bacon, crisply cooked and crumbled
- 0.7-oz. pkg. of Italian salad dressing mix
- 1 cup of shredded mozzarella cheese

DIRECTION:

1. Combine all ingredients (excluding buns) in a large-sized mixing dish. Mix thoroughly and divide into 6 patties.
2. Preheat the Griddle at medium-high temperature and brush a thin layer of olive oil on it.
3. Cook on the Griddle till the desired level of doneness is reached for around 5 to 8 min on each side. On buns, serve.

NUTRITION: Calories 684, Fat 28g, Protein 41g, Carbs 65g

CRUNCHY CHICKEN BURGERS

Preparation Time:
10 minutes

Cooking time:
20 minutes

Servings:
4-6

INGREDIENTS:

- 1/4 cup of honey barbecue sauce
- 1/8 teaspoon of salt
- 1 lb. of ground chicken
- 3/4 cup of mini shredded wheat cereal, crushed
- 4 to 6 hamburger buns, split
- 1 egg, beaten
- 1/8 teaspoon of pepper

DIRECTION:

1. Combine all ingredients, except for the buns, and shape into 4 to 6 patties.
2. Preheat the Griddle at medium-high temperature and brush a thin layer of olive oil on it.
3. Cook for around 5 to 6 min per side, or till the center is no longer pink. On buns, serve alongside your favorite sauces and toppings.

NUTRITION: Calories 566, Fat 28g, Protein 41g, Carbs 38g

TURKEY SANDWICH

 Preparation Time: 10 minutes

 Cooking time: 10 minutes

 Servings: 1

INGREDIENTS:

- 3 oz. of turkey breast, cooked and shredded
- 1 cheese slice
- 2 bread slices
- 1 tablespoon of mayonnaise

DIRECTION:

1. Apply mayonnaise to one side of each bread slice.
2. Top 1 slice of bread with turkey & cheese
3. Cover with the last slice of bread.
4. Preheat your Griddle to medium-high. The Griddle should be oiled thinly.
5. Coat the top of the Griddle using cooking spray.
6. Cook the sandwich for around 5 min on a heated griddle top or till golden brown on both sides.
7. Enjoy your meal.

NUTRITION: Calories 307, Fat 16g, Protein 23g, Carbs 16g

BEAN & CHILE BURGERS

Preparation Time:
10 minutes

Cooking time:
20 minutes

Servings:
4

INGREDIENTS:

- 4-oz. can of green chilies
- 1/2 cup of cornmeal
- 1/4 teaspoon of garlic powder
- 16-oz. drained and rinsed black beans
- 11-oz. can of corn, drained
- 4 sandwich buns, split
- 1 cup of cooked rice
- 1 teaspoon of onion powder
- salt to taste
- Optional: salsa

DIRECTION:

1. Preheat the Griddle at medium-high temperature and brush a thin layer of olive oil on it.
2. In a large-sized mixing bowl, mash the beans, then add the corn, onion powder, chilies, rice, cornmeal, and garlic powder. Form the mixture into four big patties and season using salt. Add the patties to the Griddle and cook till golden brown on both sides, around 4 to 5 min on each side.
3. Serve on buns with salsa on the side, if desired.

NUTRITION: Calories 433, Fat 27g, Protein 13g, Carbs 36g

BACON AND VENISON BURGERS

Preparation Time:
15 minutes

Cooking time:
10 minutes

Servings:
5

INGREDIENTS:

- 1 lb. peppercorn bacon, diced
- 5 lbs. ground venison
- 2 cups breadcrumbs
- 1/2 cup Worcestershire sauce
- 1/4 cup evaporated milk
- Five cloves garlic, minced
- 1 tsp ground cayenne pepper

DIRECTION:

1. Preheat an outdoor griddle for medium-high heat.
2. Put bacon in a stainless-steel jar; include venison, breadcrumbs, Worcestershire sauce, garlic, milk, and cayenne pepper.
3. Mix venison mix with your hands and shape into 5-ounce balls.
4. Press chunks with the rear of one dish to make patties.
5. Cook patties until the desired doneness is reached, about 5 minutes on each side.
6. An instant-read thermometer inserted into the middle must see at least 160 degrees F (70 degrees C).

NUTRITION: Calories: 823, Fat: 24.8 g, Cholesterol: 354 mg, Carb: 39.3-g, Protein: 103.5 g

BRUNCH BURGER

Preparation Time: 10 minutes	**Cooking time:** 10 minutes	**Servings:** 2

INGREDIENTS:

- Lean ground chuck beef (6-ozs, 170-gms)
- 4 rashers bacon, cooked until crispy
- Salt and black pepper Olive oil
- Two burger buns
- 2 slices of American cheese
- 2 medium eggs, fried
- 2 hash browns, cooked and kept warm

DIRECTION:

1. Split the steak into 2 parts and shape it into lean, actually patties—season with salt and black pepper.
2. Coat the top of the Griddle using cooking spray.
3. Cook for 3-4 minutes on each side until cooked to your taste.
4. Have the hamburgers off the hot griddle top and put each into a bun.
5. Top each patty with a slice of bacon, and cheese, followed by a fried egg and hash brown.
6. Serve right away.

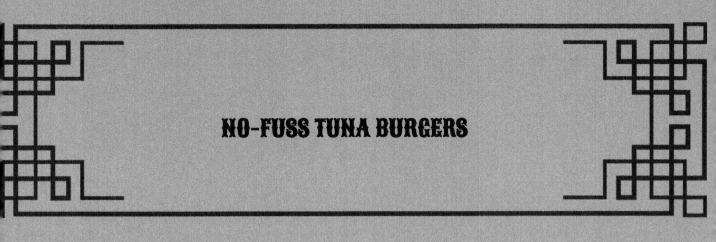

NO-FUSS TUNA BURGERS

Preparation Time:
15 minutes

Cooking time:
15 minutes

Servings:
6

INGREDIENTS:

- 2 lb. tuna steak
- 1 green bell pepper, seeded and chopped
- 1 white onion, chopped
- 2 eggs
- 1 Tsp. soy sauce
- 1 Tbsp. blackened Saskatchewan rub
- Salt and ground black pepper

DIRECTIONS:

1. Set the griddle temperature to 500 degrees F and preheat for 15 minutes.
2. Stir the remaining ingredients in a small bowl.
3. With greased hands, make patties from the mixture.
4. Place the patties onto the griddle top and cook for about 10-15 minutes, flipping once halfway through.
5. Serve hot.

NUTRITION: Calories: 313, Carbohydrates: 3.4g, Protein: 47.5g, Fat: 11g, Sugar: 1.9g, Sodium: 174mg, Fiber: 0.7g .

RUBS

MONTREAL STEAK RUB

 Preparation Time: 5 minutes

 Cooking time: 0 minutes

 Servings: 8

INGREDIENTS:

- 2 Tbsp. Salt - 2 Tbsp. cracked black pepper
- 2 Tbsp. Paprika - 1 Tbsp. red pepper flakes
- Tbsp. Coriander - 1 Tbsp. dill
- 1 Tbsp. garlic powder
- 1 Tbsp. onion powder

DIRECTIONS:

1. Stir well to combine all ingredients with an airtight jar, then cover. Consume within 6 months.

NUTRITION: Calories: 19, Fat: 0.5g, Carbs: 3g, Protein: 1g

QUICK ROSEMARY GARLIC RUB

Preparation Time:
5 minutes

Cooking time:
0 minutes

Servings:
4

INGREDIENTS:

- 1 tablespoon ground black pepper
- 1 tablespoon dried rosemary
- 8 cloves garlic
- 1/3 cup olive oil
- 1 tablespoon kosher salt
- 3 tablespoons chopped fresh rosemary

DIRECTIONS:

1. Take a little bowl and merge fresh rosemary, kosher salt, black pepper, garlic, and dried rosemary. Just slowly stir in olive oil to make a thick paste. Now, rub it into the meat before cooking.

NUTRITION: Calories: 489kcal, Carbs: 21.3g, Fat: 12g, Protein: 24g

STEAK MARINADE

Preparation Time:
5 minutes

Cooking time:
0 minutes

Servings:
1 Cups

INGREDIENTS:

- 1 Tbsp. Worcestershire sauce
- 2 Tbsp. Red wine vinegar
- 1/2 cup barbeque sauce
- 3 Tbsp. soy sauce
- 1/4 cup steak sauce
- 1 clove garlic
- 1 Tsp. Mustard
- Pepper and salt to taste

DIRECTION:

1. Set all the ingredients in a bowl and mix thoroughly.
2. Use immediately or keep refrigerated.

NUTRITION: Calories: 303kcal, Carbs: 42g, Fat: 10g, Protein: 2.4g

PERUVIAN CHICKEN MARINADE

Preparation Time:
5 minutes

Cooking time:
0 minutes

Servings:
1

INGREDIENTS:

- 3 tablespoons olive oil
- 1/4 cup lime juice
- 4 cloves garlic
- 1 tablespoon salt
- 2 teaspoons paprika
- 1 teaspoon black pepper
- 1 tablespoon ground cumin
- 1 teaspoon dried oregano
- 2 teaspoons sugar

DIRECTION:

1. Use the food processor device to combine all ingredients and pulse until you have a smooth paste.
2. To use: spread the marinade on a whole chicken or chicken piece. Make sure to work the marinade under the chicken skin for the best flavor. Use the remaining sauce to baste the chicken as you cook.

NUTRITION: Calories: 101, Sodium: 2mg, Dietary Fiber: 0.7g, Fat: 0.1g, Carbs: 27.2g, Protein: 0.3g

GRAPEFRUIT JUICE MARINADE

Preparation Time:
25 minutes

Cooking time:
0 minutes

Servings:
3 Cups

INGREDIENTS:

- 1/2 reduced-sodium soy sauce
- 3 cups grapefruit juice, unsweetened
- 1-1/2 lb. Chicken, bone, and skin removed
- 1/4 brown sugar

DIRECTION:

1. Thoroughly mix all your ingredients in a large bowl.
2. Add the chicken and allow it to marinate for 2-3 hours before cooking.

NUTRITION: Calories: 489kcal, Carbs: 21.3g, Fat: 12g, Protein: 24g

JERK RUB

Preparation Time:
5 minutes

Cooking time:
0 minutes

Servings:
1/3 Cup

INGREDIENTS:

- 2 tablespoons dried onion flakes
- 1 tablespoon dried thyme
- 2 teaspoons ground allspice
- 2 teaspoons black pepper
- 1/2 teaspoon ground cinnamon
- 1/2 teaspoon cayenne pepper
- 1 teaspoon salt
- Vegetable oil

DIRECTION:

1. In a small bowl, combine the onion, thyme, allspice, pepper, cinnamon, cayenne pepper, and salt. Mix well.
2. To use: coat your meat in oil and then rub a generous amount of spice blend into the heart. Let it cool before cooking.

NUTRITION: Calories: 394, Sodium: 2038mg, Dietary Fiber: 0.9g, Fat: 9.6g, Carbs: 75.8g, Protein: 2.4g

CLASSIC CAJUN RUB

Preparation Time:
10 minutes

Cooking time:
0 minutes

Servings:
3 tablespoons

INGREDIENTS:

- 1 teaspoon freshly ground black pepper
- 1 teaspoon onion powder
- 1 teaspoon coarse kosher salt
- 1 teaspoon garlic powder
- 1 teaspoon sweet paprika
- 1/2 teaspoon cayenne pepper
- 1/2 teaspoon red pepper flakes
- 1/2 teaspoon dried oregano leaves
- 1/2 teaspoon dried thyme
- 1/2 teaspoon smoked paprika

DIRECTIONS:

1. You can use a zip-top bag or container that stays airtight to combine the black pepper, onion powder, salt, garlic powder, sweet paprika, cayenne, red pepper flakes, oregano, thyme, and smoked paprika.
2. Close the container and shake to mix. The unused rub will keep in an airtight container for months.

NUTRITION: Calories: 62., Carbs: 15.9g, Fat: 0.3g, Protein: 0.1g

COFFEE MEAT RUB

Preparation Time:
5 minutes

Cooking time:
3 minutes

Servings:
8

INGREDIENTS:

- Tbsp. coffee beans, ground
- 2 Tbsp. black pepper, ground
- 1/2 Tbsp. kosher salt
- 1/2 Tsp. cayenne pepper
- 1 Tbsp. cumin, ground

DIRECTIONS:

1. Dry fry the coffee in a roasting pan over medium heat until it releases fragrance.
2. Using a container, mix the coffee, black pepper, kosher salt, cayenne pepper, and ground cumin.
3. Use the rub on the steak before cooking.

NUTRITION: Calories: 10, Sodium: 320mg, Carbs: 2g

CAJUN CHICKEN RUB

Preparation Time:
5 minutes

Cooking time:
0 minutes

Servings:
8

INGREDIENTS:

- 2 Tbsp. Onion powder - 1 Tsp. dried Oregano
- 2 Tbsp. Cayenne pepper - 2 Tsp. Paprika
- 2 Tsp. Garlic powder - 6 Tbsp. Louisiana-style hot Marinade
- 2 Tsp. Lawry's seasoning salt
- Tsp. Black pepper
- 1 Tsp. dried thyme

DIRECTIONS:

1. Combine all ingredients in an airtight jar, stir well, then seal.
2. Use within six months.

NUTRITION : Calories: 5, Carbs: 1g

MEMPHIS RUB

Preparation Time:
5 minutes

Cooking time:
0 minutes

Servings:
8

INGREDIENTS:

- 1/2 cup (55g) paprika
- 1/4 cup (40g) garlic powder
- 1/4 cup (30g) mild chili powder
- 3 Tbsp. salt
- 3 Tbsp. black pepper
- 2 Tbsp. onion powder
- 2 Tbsp. celery seeds
- Tbsp. brown sugar
- 1 Tbsp. dried oregano
- 1 Tbsp. dried thyme
- 1 Tbsp. cumin
- Tsp. dry mustard
- Tsp. ground coriander
- 2 Tsp. ground allspice

DIRECTIONS:

1. Combine all ingredients in an airtight jar, stir well, then seal.
2. Use within six months.

NUTRITION: Calories: 50, Fat: 0.3g, Carbs: 13g

PORK

BABY BACK RIBS

Preparation Time:
10 minutes

Cooking time:
2 Hours

Servings:
6

INGREDIENTS:

- 3 racks of baby back ribs
- Salt and pepper to taste

DIRECTIONS:

1. Clean the ribs by removing the extra membrane that covers them. Pat dries the ribs with a clean paper towel. Whisk the baby's back ribs with salt and pepper to taste. Cook at least four hours after resting in the fridge.
2. Once ready to cook, fire your Griddle to 225F and preheat for 15 minutes.
3. Cook for two hours. Carefully flip the ribs halfway through the cooking time for even cooking.

NUTRITION: Calories: 1037, Protein: 92.5g, Carbs: 1.4g, Fat: 73.7g, Sugar: 0.2g

CITRUS-BRINED PORK ROAST

Preparation Time: 10 minutes	**Cooking time:** 45 minutes	**Servings:** 6

INGREDIENTS:

- 1/2 cup of salt
- 1/4 cup brown sugar
- 3 cloves of garlic, minced
- 2 dried bay leaves
- 6 peppercorns
- 1 lemon, juiced
- 1/2 teaspoon dried fennel seeds
- 1/2 teaspoon red pepper flakes
- 1/2 cup of apple juice
- 1/2 cup of orange juice
- 5 pounds of pork loin
- 2 tablespoons extra virgin olive oil

DIRECTIONS:

1. Mix together the salt, brown sugar, garlic, bay leaves, peppercorns, lemon juice, fennel seeds, pepper flakes, apple juice, and orange juice in a bowl.
2. Mix to form a paste rub.
3. Rub the mixture onto the pork loin and marinate for at least 2 hours in the fridge. Add in the oil.
4. When ready to cook, fire the Griddle to 300F and preheat for 15 minutes.
5. Place the seasoned pork loin on the griddle top.
6. Cook for 45 minutes.
7. Flip the pork halfway through the cooking process.

NUTRITION: Calories: 869; Protein: 97.2g; Carbs: 15.2g; Fat: 43.9g, Sugar: 13g

PINEAPPLE PORK BBQ

Preparation Time:
10 minutes

Cooking time:
60 minutes

Servings:
4

INGREDIENTS:

- 1-Pound Pork Sirloin
- 4 Cups Pineapple Juice
- 3 cloves of Garlic, Minced
- 1 Cup Carne Aside Marinade
- 2 Tablespoons Salt
- 1 Teaspoon Ground Black pepper

DIRECTIONS:

1. Place all ingredients in a bowl. Massage the pork sirloin to coat with all elements. Marinate for at least two hours in the fridge.
2. When ready to cook, fire the Griddle to 300F and preheat for 15 minutes.
3. Place the pork sirloin on a hot griddle top and cook for 45 to 60 minutes. Flip the pork halfway through the cooking process.
4. At the same time, when you put the pork on the hot griddle top, place the marinade in a pan and place it inside the Griddle. Allow the marinade to cook and reduce.
5. Baste the pork sirloin with the reduced marinade before the cooking time ends.
6. Allow resting before slicing.

NUTRITION: Calories: 347; Protein: 33.4 g; Carbs: 45.8 g; Fat: 4.2g, Sugar: 36g

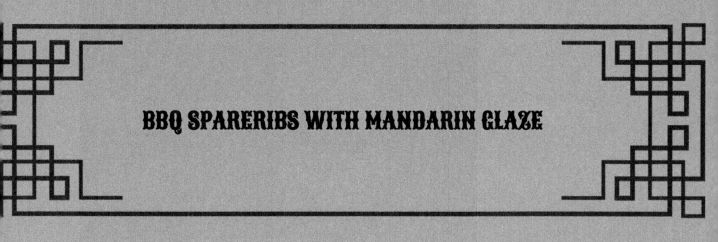

BBQ SPARERIBS WITH MANDARIN GLAZE

Preparation Time:
10 minutes

Cooking time:
1 Hour

Servings:
6

INGREDIENTS:

- 3 large spareribs, membrane removed
- 3 tablespoons yellow mustard
- 1 tablespoon Worcestershire sauce
- 1 cup honey
- 1 1/2 cup brown sugar
- 13 ounces Trailer Mandarin Glaze
- 1 teaspoon sesame oil
- 1 teaspoon soy sauce
- 1 teaspoon garlic powder

DIRECTIONS:

1. Place the spareribs on a working surface and carefully remove the connective tissue membrane that covers the ribs.
2. Set the rest of the ingredients until well combined in a bowl.
3. Massage the spice mixture onto the spareribs. At least 3 hours should be allowed to rest in the fridge.
4. When ready to cook, fire the Griddle to 300F and preheat for 15 minutes.
5. Place the seasoned ribs on the hot griddle top.
6. Cook for 60 minutes.
7. Once cooked, allow resting before slicing.

NUTRITION: Calories: 1263; Protein: 36.9g; Carbs: 110.3g; Fat: 76.8g, Sugar: 107g

PORK SAUSAGES

Preparation Time: 10 minutes	**Cooking time:** 1 Hour	**Servings:** 6

INGREDIENTS:

- 3 pounds of ground pork
- 1/2 tablespoon ground mustard
- 1 tablespoon onion powder
- 1 tablespoon garlic powder
- 1 teaspoon pink curing salt
- 1 teaspoon salt
- 1 teaspoon black pepper
- 1/4 cup of ice water
- Hog casings, soaked & rinsed in cold water

DIRECTIONS:

1. Combine all ingredients except the hog casings in a bowl. Mix with your hands until evenly combined.
2. Pack the pork mixture into the hog casings using a sausage stuffer.
3. Roll the stuffed hog casing into a sausage by measuring 4 inches. Make sausage links by repeating that process.
4. When ready to cook, fire the Griddle to 225F and preheat for 15 minutes.
5. Place the sausage links on the hot griddle top and cook for 1 hour or until the sausage's internal temperature reads 155F.
6. Allow resting before slicing.

NUTRITION: Calories: 688; Protein: 58.9g; Carbs: 2.7g; Fat: 47.3g, Sugar: 0.2g

BASTED STEAK

Preparation Time:
5 minutes

Cooking time:
8 minutes

Servings:
4

INGREDIENTS:

- Four tablespoons of melted butter
- Two tablespoons of Worcestershire sauce
- Two tablespoons of Dijon mustard
- Trailer Prime Rib Rub, as needed
- Two porterhouse steaks, 1 1/2 inch thick

DIRECTIONS:

1. In a bowl, mix the butter, Worcestershire sauce, mustard, and Prime Rib Rub.
2. Massage all over the steak on all sides. Allow steak to rest for an hour before cooking.
3. When ready to cook, fire the Griddle to 500F.
4. Set the steaks on a hot griddle top and cook for 4 minutes on each side or until the internal temperature reads 130F for medium-rare steaks.
5. Take away from the hot griddle top and allow resting for 5 minutes before slicing.

NUTRITION: Calories: 515, Protein: 65.3g, Carbs: 2.1g, Fat: 27.7g, Sugar: 0.9g

PORK BURNT ENDS

Preparation Time:
15 minutes

Cooking time:
4 hours 30 minutes

Servings:
10

INGREDIENTS:

- 4 pounds of pork belly
- 4 Tbsp. brown sugar
- 1/4 Tsp. cayenne pepper
- 1 Tsp. red pepper flakes
- 1/2 Tsp. onion powder
- 1/2 Tsp. garlic powder
- 1 Tbsp. paprika
- 1 Tsp. oregano
- 1 Tbsp. freshly ground black pepper
- 2 Tbsp. salt or to taste
- 1 Tsp. dried peppermint
- 2 Tbsp. olive oil
- 1/4 cup butter
- 1 cup BBQ sauce
- 4 Tbsp. maple syrup
- 2 Tbsp. chopped fresh parsley

DIRECTIONS:

1. Trim pork belly of any excess fat and cut off silver skin. Cut the pork into 1/2-inch cubes.
2. To make the rub, combine the sugar, cayenne, pepper flakes, onion powder, garlic, paprika, oregano, black pepper, salt, and peppermint in a mixing bowl.
3. Drizzle oil over the pork and season each pork cube generously with the rub.
4. Preheat your Griddle to 205°F for 15 minutes.
5. Arrange the pork chunks onto the griddle top and cook for about 3 hours, or until the pork chunks turn dark red.
6. Meanwhile, combine the BBQ sauce, maple syrup, and butter in an aluminum pan.
7. Remove the pork slices from heat and put them in the pan with the sauce. Stir to combine.
8. Cover the pan tightly w/ aluminum foil and place it on a hot griddle top. The pork needs to reach 200°F after 1 hour of cooking.
9. Remove the pork from heat & let it sit for some minutes.
10. Serve and garnish with fresh chopped parsley.

NUTRITION: Calories: 477, Fat: 41.8g, Cholesterol: 58mg, Carbohydrate: 19.3g, Protein:

PORK KEBABS

Preparation Time:
10 minutes

Cooking time:
12 minutes

Servings:
4

INGREDIENTS:

- 1 pork tenderloin (cut into 2-inch cubes)
- 1 large bell pepper (sliced)
- 1 large yellow bell pepper (sliced)
- 1 large green bell pepper (sliced)
- 1 onion (sliced)
- 10 medium cremains mushrooms (esteemed and halved)
- Wooden (soaked in water for 30 minutes. at least)
- Marinade:
- 1/2 cup olive oil
- 1/2 Tsp. pepper
- 1 Tsp. salt
- 1 Tbsp. freshly chopped parsley
- 3 Tbsp. brown sugar
- 2 Tsp. Dijon mustard
- 3 Tbsp. soy sauce
- 1 lemon (juice)
- 1 Tbsp. freshly chopped thyme
- 1 Tsp. minced garlic

DIRECTIONS:

1. Mix marinade ingredients in a large bowl.
2. Add the pork and mushroom and toss to combine.
3. Cover the bowl tightly w/ aluminum foil and refrigerate for 8 hours.
4. Remove the mushroom and pork from the marinade.
5. Thread the bell peppers, onion, mushroom, and pork onto skewers to make kabobs.
6. Preheat your Griddle to high for 15 minutes.
7. Arrange the kebobs onto the hot griddle top and cook for 12 minutes, 6 minutes per side, or until the pork's internal temperature reaches 145°F.
8. Remove kebabs from heat.

NUTRITION: Calories: 272, Fat: 15.8g, Cholesterol: 62mg, Carbohydrate: 9.2g, Protein: 24g

SAUSAGES

Preparation Time:
15 minutes

Cooking time:
3 hours

Servings:
4

INGREDIENTS:

- 3 pounds of ground pork
- 1 tablespoon onion powder
- 1 tablespoon garlic powder
- 1 teaspoon curing salt
- 4 teaspoon black pepper
- 1/2 tablespoon salt
- 1/2 tablespoon ground mustard
- Hog casings, soaked
- 1/2 cup ice water

DIRECTIONS:

1. Take a medium bowl, place all the ingredients in it except for water and hog casings, and stir until well mixed.
2. Pour in water, stir until incorporated, place the mixture in a sausage stuffer, then stuff the hog casings and tie the link to the desired length.
3. When the Griddle has preheated, place the sausage links on the griddle top, shut the Griddle, and cook for around 5 min on each side on a hot griddle top or until the internal temperature reaches 155° F.
4. Transfer sausages to a dish; let them rest for 5 minutes, then slice and serve.

NUTRITION: Calories: 230, Fat: 22 g, Carbs: 2 g, Protein: 14 g

HONEY CURED HAM RIBS

Preparation Time: 30 minutes

Cooking time: 4 hours

Servings: 3

INGREDIENT:

- 3/4 cup of honey
- 1-1/2 cup of cold water
- 1-1/2 cup of hot water
- 8 cloves
- 1 rack of spareribs
- 3/4 cup of kosher or sea salt
- 1-1/2 Tsp. of pink curing salt
- 3 bay leaves
- Mustard seed caviar

DIRECTIONS:

1. Place the ribs on the baking sheet. Mix the hot water, honey, coarse salt, and pink curing salt until the salt and honey dissolve in the water. Allow it to cool to room temperature.
2. Add the rib to the cooled brine and transfer it to a Ziploc bag. Keep in the refrigerator for 3 days.
3. Prepare a baking pan by removing the ribs from the refrigerator.
4. Preheat the Griddle for 15 minutes at 250°F.
5. Put the ribs on the hot griddle top and cook for around 5 min on each side.
6. Serve immediately with mustard seed caviar.

NUTRITION: Calories: 375kcal, Protein: 45g, Fat: 43.5g, Carbs: 55g

HONEY SOY PORK CHOPS

Preparation Time:
10-25 minutes

Cooking time:
25 minutes

Servings:
6

INGREDIENTS:

- 6 (4 ounces) boneless pork chops
- 1/4 cup organic honey
- 1 to 2 tbsp. low sodium soy sauce
- 2 tbsp. olive oil
- 1 tbsp. rice mirin

DIRECTIONS:

1. Whisk together the honey, soy sauce, oil, and white vinegar until everything is well-combined. Place the pork chops and dressing in a big sealable plastic bag and set aside for 1 hour to marinate.
2. Preheat the Griddle to medium-high heat and cook the pork chops for 4 to 5 minutes, or until they readily release from the grill, turning once or twice. For the other side, cook for 5 more minutes, or until the internal temperature reaches 145°F.
3. Prepare the dish and serve it to your guests.

NUTRITION: Calories: 399, Fat: 6.8 g, Cholesterol: 238 mg, Carb: 7.7-g, Protein: 65.9 g

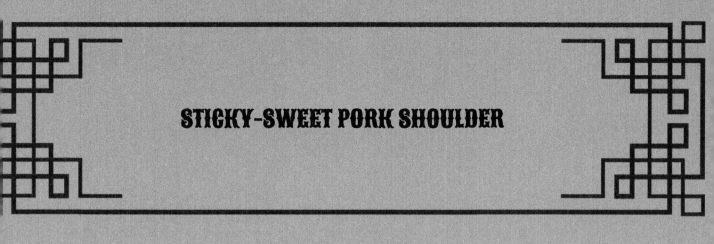

STICKY-SWEET PORK SHOULDER

Preparation Time:
25 minutes

Cooking time:
8 minutes

Servings:
8

INGREDIENTS:

- 1 (5 lbs.) Boston Butt pork shoulder
- For the marinade: 2 tbsp. garlic, minced
- 1 large piece ginger, peeled and chopped
- 1 cup hoisin sauce
- ¾ cup fish sauce
- 2/3 cup honey
- 2/3 cup Shaoxing
- ½ cup chili oil
- 1/3 cup oyster sauce
- 1/3 cup sesame oil
- For the glaze: ¾ cup dark brown sugar
- 1 tbsp. light molasses

DIRECTIONS:

1. To prepare the pork shoulder, place it on a cutting board with the flat side down and the short end facing you. Make a shallow incision along the whole length of one long side of the shoulder with a long sharp knife held approximately 1"–112" above the cutting board using a long sharp knife. Continue to cut further into the flesh, raising and unfurling the meat with your free hand until it rests flat on the cutting board. Marinate in a blender until smooth (save 12 cups for the glaze).
2. For 2 hours minimum, cover and chill the mixture. The leftover marinade should be placed in a large zip-top plastic bag and sealed. Marinate the pork shoulder for 8 hours in a zip-top bag in the refrigerator. Start by preheating the Griddle over medium heat (the thermometer should read 350° when you shut the lid).
3. Remove the pork from the marinade, allowing any extra liquid to drop out. In a separate bowl, whisk the glaze ingredients until the sugar is completely dissolved.
4. For 8 minutes on a hot grill, basting and rotating with tongs every minute or two until the pork is well-coated with sauce and slightly browned on the edges.
5. When the meat thermometer registers 145°F when inserted into the thickest part of the meat, cut into 1" thick slices against the grain on a cutting board and serve.

NUTRITION: Calories: 764, Fat: 55g, Carbohydrates: 2g, Protein: 63g

ROSEMARY DIJON PORK CHOPS

 Preparation Time: 25 minutes

 Cooking time: 10 minutes

 Servings: 4

INGREDIENTS:

- 4 pork chops, boneless
- 2 tbsp. fresh rosemary, chopped
- 1/4 cup Dijon mustard
- 1/4 cup coconut aminos
- 2 tbsp. olive oil
- 1/2 tsp. salt

DIRECTIONS:

1. Combine the rosemary, coconut aminos, olive oil, Dijon mustard, and salt in a large mixing bowl. Pork chops should be added to the basin and coated well. Refrigerate for 1 hour after covering with plastic wrap. Preheat the Griddle to a high heat setting before you begin. Cooking spray should be sprayed onto the griddle top.
2. Grill the marinated pork chops until they are crispy and brown on each side for 5 minutes. Prepare the dish and serve it to your guests

NUTRITION: Calories: 309, Cal Fat: 7 g, Carbohydrates: 20 g, Protein: 34 g, Fiber: 1 g

BEEF

BEEF TACOS

Preparation Time:
5 minutes

Cooking time:
15 minutes

Servings:
5

INGREDIENTS:

- 1 lb ground beef
- 1 cup medium hot salsa
- Sour Cream
- Corn Tortillas
- Shredded lettuce
- 1 tablespoon taco seasoning
- Shredded Cheese
- Fresh Roma tomatoes (diced)

DIRECTIONS:

1. Brown ground beef with taco seasoning and medium hot salsa. It tastes fantastic when cooked in salsa.
2. Place your corn tortillas on your griddle that has been heated. If you want them extra crispy, use butter to grease the griddle.
3. On the tortilla, place a tiny handful of shredded cheese and top with cooked ground beef.
4. Allow to heat until the tortilla is crispy.
5. Add shredded lettuce, tomatoes, sour cream, and other ingredients to taste.
6. Fold taco over with spatula and cook for a few minutes more until it keeps its shape.

NUTRITION: Calories: 210, Carbs: 20g, Fat: 10g, Protein: 10g

HERBED BEEF EYE FILLET

Preparation Time: 30 minutes

Cooking time: 10 minutes

Servings: 6

INGREDIENTS:

- Pepper
- Salt
- 2 tablespoons chopped rosemary
- 2 tablespoons chopped basil
- 2 tablespoons olive oil
- 3 cloves crushed garlic
- 1/4 cup chopped oregano
- 1/4 cup chopped parsley
- 2 pounds beef eye fillet

DIRECTIONS:

1. Use salt and pepper to rub in the meat before placing it in a container.
2. Place the garlic, oil, rosemary, oregano, basil, and parsley in a bowl. Stir well to combine.
3. Rub the fillet generously with this mixture on all sides. For 30 minutes, leave the meat on the counter.
4. Preheat your Griddle at medium-high temperature.
5. Coat the top of the Griddle using cooking spray.
6. Cook for around 5 min on each side on a hot griddle or your preferred tenderness.
7. Once it is done to your likeness, allow it to rest for ten minutes. Slice and enjoy.

NUTRITION: Calories: 202, Carbs: 0g, Fat: 8g, Protein: 33g

BALSAMIC VINEGAR MOLASSES STEAK

Preparation Time: 15 minutes	**Cooking time:** 20 minutes	**Servings:** 4

INGREDIENTS:

- Pepper
- Salt
- 1 tablespoon balsamic vinegar
- 2 tablespoons molasses
- 1 tablespoon red wine vinegar
- 1 cup beef broth
- 2 1/2 pounds steak of choice

DIRECTIONS:

1. Lay the steaks in a zip-top bag.
2. Add the balsamic vinegar, red wine vinegar, molasses, and beef broth to a bowl. Combine thoroughly by stirring.
3. On the top of the steaks, drizzle this mixture.
4. Place into the refrigerator for eight hours.
5. Preheat your Griddle at medium-high temperature.
6. Take the flounced steaks out of the refrigerator 30 minutes before you are ready to cook.
7. Cook on a hot griddle for 5 minutes on each side, or until the meat is tender.
8. Place onto plates and let them rest for ten minutes.

NUTRITION: Calories: 164, Carbs: 6g, Fat: 5g, Protein: 22

SPICED BRISKET

Preparation Time: 10 minutes	**Cooking time:** 9 hours	**Servings:** 8

INGREDIENTS:

- 2 tablespoons onion powder
- 2 tablespoons garlic powder
- 2 teaspoons chili powder
- 2 tablespoons paprika
- 1/3 cup coarse ground black pepper
- 1/3 cup Jacobsen salt
- Brisket:
- 1 (12 to 14 pounds / 5.4 to 6.4 kg) whole packer brisket, trimmed
- 1 1/2 cup beef broth

DIRECTIONS:

1. Thoroughly put all the rub ingredients. Season the brisket with the rub on all sides.
2. When ready to cook, set griddle temperature to 225°F (107°C) and preheat for 15 minutes.
3. Place the brisket, fat-side down, on the griddle top and cook for about 5 to 6 hours.
4. Take out the brisket and wrap it in a double layer of foil, then add the beef broth to the foil packet.
5. Return the foiled brisket to the Griddle and cook for about another 3 hours.
6. Take out the brisket and unwrap it from the foil. Allow resting for 15 minutes.

NUTRITION: Calories: 200, Carbs: 0g, Fat: 7g, Protein: 33g

BISON TOMAHAWK STEAK

Preparation Time:
5 minutes

Cooking time:
12 minutes

Servings:
4

INGREDIENTS:

- 2 1/2 whole bone-in buffalo rib-eye steak
- Two teaspoons of cherry wood smoked salt
- 1 1/2 tablespoon black pepper

DIRECTIONS:

1. Fire the Griddle to 450F and heat up for 15 minutes.
2. Salt and pepper the rib-eye steak to taste.
3. Take the steak on the hot griddle top.
4. Cook until the internal temperature reaches 140F.
5. Take it out from the Griddle and let it rest before slicing.

NUTRITION: Calories: 751, Protein: 51.6g, Carbs: 1.7g, Fat: 60.1g, Sugar: 0.02g

BAKED VENISON MEATLOAF

Preparation Time:
10 minutes

Cooking time:
30 minutes

Servings:
6

INGREDIENTS:

- 2 pounds venison, ground
- 1-pound pork, ground
- 1 cup breadcrumbs
- 1 cup milk
- Two tablespoons onion, diced
- Three tablespoons salt
- One tablespoon of black pepper
- 1/2 tablespoon thyme
- 1 1/2 pounds parsnips, chopped
- 1 1/2 pounds of russet potatoes, chopped
- 1/4 cup butter

DIRECTIONS:

1. Fire the Griddle to 500F and heat up for 15 minutes.
2. Combine all ingredients in a bowl.
3. Grease a loaf pan and place the mixture in it.
4. Place on the hot griddle top and cook until the internal temperature reads 160F.

NUTRITION: Calories: 668, Protein: 70.4g, Carbs: 45.7 g, Fat: 22g, Sugar: 8.7g

SWEETHEART STEAK

 Preparation Time: 5 minutes

 Cooking time: 15 minutes

 Servings: 1

INGREDIENTS:

- 20 ounces boneless strip steak, butterflied
- 2 ounces pure sea salt
- 2 teaspoons black pepper
- 2 tablespoons raw dark chocolate, finely chopped
- 1/2 tablespoon extra-virgin olive oil

DIRECTIONS:

1. On a cutting board, trim the meat into a heart shape using a sharp knife. Set aside.
2. In a lighter bowl, combine the rest of the fixings to create a spice rub mix.
3. Rub onto the steak and massage until well-seasoned.
4. When ready to cook, fire your Griddle to 450F.
5. For each side of the steak, cook for 7 minutes.
6. Allow resting for 5 minutes before slicing.

NUTRITION: Calories: 727, Protein: 132.7g, Carbs: 8.8 g, Fat: 18.5g, Sugar: 5.2g

BEEF JERKY

Preparation Time:
15 minutes

Cooking time:
5 minutes

Servings:
10

INGREDIENTS:

- 3 pounds of sirloin steaks
- 2 cups soy sauce
- 1 cup pineapple juice
- 1/2 cup brown sugar
- 2 Tbsp. sriracha
- 2 Tbsp. hoisin
- 2 Tbsp. red pepper flake
- 2 Tbsp. rice wine vinegar
- 2 Tbsp. onion powder

DIRECTIONS:

1. Set the marinade in a zip lock bag and add the beef. Mix until well coated and remove as much air as possible.
2. Set the bag in a fridge and let marinate overnight or for 6 hours. Remove the bag from the fridge an hour before cooking
3. Preheat your Griddle at medium-high temperature.
4. Lay the meat on a hot griddle top, leaving a half-inch space between the pieces. Let cool for 5 hours and turn after 2 hours.
5. Remove from the Griddle and let cool. Serve or refrigerate

NUTRITION: Calories: 309, Cal Fat: 7 g, Carbohydrates: 20 g, Protein: 34 g, Fiber: 1 g

SLUM DUNK BRISKET

Preparation Time: 20 minutes	**Cooking time:** 9 hours minutes	**Servings:** 9

INGREDIENTS:

- 1/4 cup of pickle juice, dill
- Kosher or sea salt
- Barbecue sauce
- 1/4 cup of mustard, Dijon
- 6 pounds of brisket
- 6 strips of bacon, artisanal
- Black pepper

DIRECTIONS:

1. Preheat the Griddle to 250°F.
2. In a bowl, combine the pickle juice and mustard. Trim off the fats on the brisket, then rub the mustard mixture on it—season with salt and pepper. Put bacon on the brisket.
3. Place the coated brisket and bacon directly on a hot griddle, and cook until the internal temperature reads 160°F.
4. Remove the brisket from the hot griddle top when it is ready.

NUTRITION: Calories: 355.3kcal, Fat: 47.2g, Protein: 30.9g, Carbs: 41g

CHERRY SMOKED STRIP STEAK

Preparation Time:
30 minutes

Cooking time:
2 hours 10 minutes

Servings:
3

INGREDIENTS:

- Kosher or sea salt
- Olive oil
- Black pepper
- 1-1/2 pound of rib steak

DIRECTIONS:

1. Preheat the Griddle to 225°F.
2. Salt and pepper the steak before cooking.
3. Place the seasoned steak directly on the hot griddle top and cook until the internal temperature reads 160°F.
4. Increase the temperature to high and cook it for another 10 minutes.
5. Serve it hot.

NUTRITION: Calories: 289.5kcal, Protein: 35.9g, Fat: 40.5g, Carbs: 51g

MEATY CHUCK SHORT RIBS

 Preparation Time: 20 minutes

 Cooking time: 5 hours

 Servings: 2

INGREDIENTS:

- English-cut 4-bone chunk meat throws short ribs
- 3 to 5 tbsp. Pete's Western Rub

DIRECTIONS:

1. Trim the fat top from the ribs, leaving a 1/4-inch fat, and remove any silver skin.
2. Remove the bones' membrane to season the meat appropriately by working a spoon handle under the membrane to get a piece lifted. Utilize a paper towel to snatch the membrane and force it off the bones.
3. Slather olive oil or mustard on all sides of the short rib section. Rub generously with seasoning on all sides.
4. Place the ribs bone-side down on the griddle top and cook at 225°F for 5 hours.
5. Rest the cooked short ribs under a free foil tent for 15 minutes before serving.

NUTRITION: Calories: 255kcal, Protein: 35g, Carbs: 42g, Fat: 35g.

POULTRY

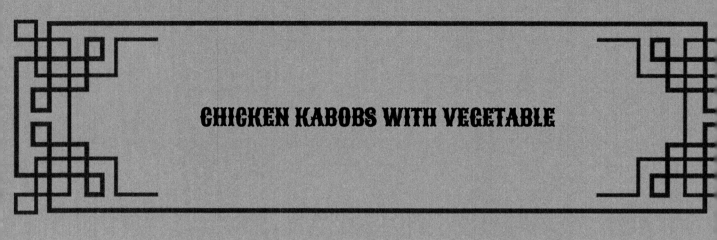

CHICKEN KABOBS WITH VEGETABLE

Preparation Time:
5 Minutes + 1 hour marinated

Cooking time:
25 minutes

Servings:
4

INGREDIENTS:

- 2 Chicken Breast, Boneless and Skinless
- 1 oz. Ranch Seasoning Packet
- 1/4 cup Olive Oil
- 1 White Onion (Small Pieces)
- 8 oz. White Mushrooms (Sliced)
- 1 Red Bell Pepper (Small Pieces)

DIRECTIONS:

1. Cut the chicken breast into 1-inch cubes.
2. Place the chicken pieces in a medium mixing basin and top with the ranch powdered seasoning packet.
3. Cover the container and refrigerate for 1 hour. Pour the olive oil over the chicken/ranch mixture and toss everything together.
4. Remove the kabobs from the fridge when you're ready to prepare them.
5. Add a layer of oil to your Griddle and preheat it at a low temperature.
6. Place the skewers on the flat top and cook the chicken kabobs slowly to avoid burning. Using a dome lid, cover the container.
7. Allow the chicken skewers to cook until golden brown on the first side. Carefully flip the kabob to the other side with a pair of tongs. Cover the skewers with the cover again. Cook until the other side is golden brown. Continue cooking until all four sides are golden brown in color and the chicken has reached a temperature of 165°F.

NUTRITION: Calories 130, Total fat 9g, Protein 10g, Carbs: 5g

CHICKEN

 Preparation Time: 10 minutes

 Cooking time: 70 minutes

 Servings: 6

INGREDIENTS:

- 5 lb. whole chicken
- 1/2 cup oil
- trigger chicken rub

DIRECTIONS:

1. Preheat the Griddle for 5 minutes and let it warm for 15 minutes or until it reaches 450.
2. To bind the chicken legs together, use baker's twine; then brush them with oil. Place the chicken on the Griddle and coat it with the rub.
3. Cook for 70 minutes or until it reaches an internal temperature of 165F.
4. Remove the chicken from the hot griddle top and let rest for 15 minutes. Cut and serve.

NUTRITION: Calories 935, Total fat 53g, Saturated fat 15g, Protein 107g, Sodium 320mg

BOURBON GLAZED TURKEY LEGS

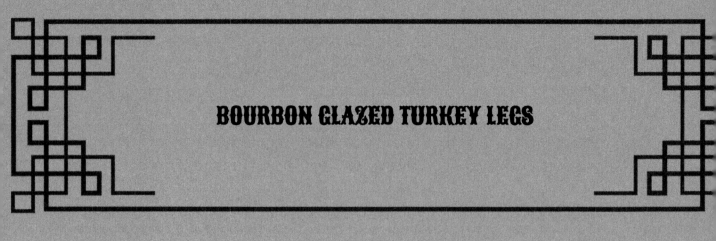

Preparation Time: 25 minutes	**Cooking time:** 2 Hours & 30 minutes	**Servings:** 12

INGREDIENTS:

- The meat
- Turkey drumsticks, fat trimmed – 6
- The brine
- Coldwater – 1 gallon
- Sugar – 1/2 cup
- Bay leaves – 2
- Thyme sprigs – 2
- Peppercorn – 6
- Salt – 1/2 cup
- The rub
- Salt and garlic powder mixture – 1/2 cup
- Olive oil – 6 tablespoons
- The glaze
- Butter, unsalted – 1/2 stick
- Chopped rosemary – 2 tablespoons
- Bourbon – 1/4 cup
- Maple syrup – 1/4 cup

DIRECTIONS:

1. Before preheating the Griddle, soak the turkey in the brine and take a large pot, add all the ingredients into it and stir until sugar and salt have dissolved.
2. Then add turkey legs to it, and let them soak for a minimum of 4 hours.
3. After 4 hours, remove turkey legs from the brine, rinse well, pat dry and then rub with salt and garlic mixture and olive oil.
4. When the Griddle has preheated, place turkey legs on the cooking rack and cook for 2 hours.
5. Meanwhile, prepare the glaze and for this, place a medium pot over medium-high heat, add butter and when it melts and begins to brown, add rosemary and cook for 1 minute.
6. Add maple syrup and bourbon, switch heat to the low level, stir until mixed and cook the sauce for 5 minutes until reduced by half and turned syrupy.
7. When turkey legs have cooked, transfer them to a pan, switch the griddle temperature to 500 degrees F, and let it preheat.
8. Return turkey legs onto the griddle rack, brush with prepared glaze and cook for 30 minutes or more until caramelized, and then the internal temperature of turkey legs reaches 165 degrees F, frequently brushing with the glaze.
9. Serve immediately.

NUTRITION: Calories: 94; Fat: 2g; Carbs: 1g; Protein: 18g

CAJUN CHICKEN BREASTS

Preparation Time:
10 minutes

Cooking time:
6 hours

Servings:
6

INGREDIENTS:

- 2 lb. skinless, boneless chicken breasts
- 2 Tbsp. Cajun seasoning
- 1 C. BBQ sauce

DIRECTIONS:

1. Set the griddle temperature and preheat for 15 minutes.
2. Apply generous amounts of Cajun seasoning to the chicken breasts.
3. Put the chicken breasts onto the hot griddle top and cook for about 4-6 hours.
4. During the last hour of cooking, coat the breasts with BBQ sauce twice.
5. Serve hot.

NUTRITION: Calories: 252, Carbohydrates: 15.1g, Protein: 33.8g, Fat: 5.5g, Sugar: 10.9g, Sodium: 570mg, Fiber: 0.3g

TURKEY BREAST

 Preparation Time: 12 Hours

 Cooking time: 20 minutes

 Servings: 6

INGREDIENTS:

- 2 pounds turkey breast, deboned
- 2 tablespoons ground black pepper
- 1/4 cup salt
- 1 cup brown sugar
- 4 cups cold water
- For The BBQ Rub:
- 2 tablespoons dried onions
- 2 tablespoons garlic powder
- 1/4 cup paprika
- 2 tablespoons ground black pepper
- 1 tablespoon salt
- 2 tablespoons brown sugar
- 2 tablespoons red chili powder
- 1 tablespoon cayenne pepper
- 2 tablespoons sugar
- 2 tablespoons ground cumin

DIRECTIONS:

1. To prepare the brine, take a large bowl, add salt, sugar, black pepper, and water, then stir until sugar is dissolved.
2. Soak the turkey breast in it for a minimum of 12 hours in the refrigerator.
3. As for the BBQ rub, you can prepare it by placing all of its ingredients in a small bowl, stirring until combined, then set aside until required.
4. Remove the turkey breast from the brine, then season generously with the BBQ rub.
5. Griddle the turkey until it reaches 160 degrees Fahrenheit.
6. Transfer the turkey to a cutting board, let it rest for 10 minutes, then slice it and serve.

NUTRITION: Calories: 250; Fat: 5 g; Carbs: 31 g; Protein: 18 g

YAN'S ROASTED QUARTERS

 Preparation Time:
20 minutes
(additional 2-4 hours marinade)

 Cooking time:
1-1.5 hours

 Servings:
4

INGREDIENTS:

- 4 fresh or thawed flounced chicken quarters
- 4-6 glasses of extra virgin olive oil
- 4 tablespoons of Yang's original dry lab

DIRECTIONS:

1. Cut off excess skin and fat chicken. Carefully peel the chicken skin and rub olive oil above and below each chicken skin.
2. When the temperature of the thickest part of the thighs and feet reaches 180 ° F and the juice becomes clear, pull the crispy chicken out of the hot Griddle.
3. Let the crispy chicken rest under a loose foil tent for 15 minutes before eating.

NUTRITION: Calories: 195, Carbs: 0g, Fat: 15g, Protein: 15g

SPATCHCOCK TURKEY

Preparation Time:
20 minutes

Cooking time:
1 hour & 20 minutes

Servings:
12 Persons

INGREDIENTS:

- 1 whole turkey (roughly 15 pounds), thawed
- Salt to taste
- 4 carrots, sliced
- 1 onion, chopped
- 5 spring's fresh thyme
- 1-quart unsalted chicken stock
- 5 spring's fresh sage
- 1-quart water
- 4 stalks of celery, chopped

DIRECTIONS:

1. Cut out the backbone using kitchen shears or a sharp knife & set it aside.
2. Lay the turkey flat on a metallic rack & generously practice the dry brine on both sides (salt). Place in a refrigerator for a single day to air dry.
3. Cook the turkey on a hot griddle top until the inner temperature displays 160 F, at 350 F.
4. Strain the turkey stock & sense free to apply it to the gravy. Serve warm and enjoy.

NUTRITION: Calories: 94; Fat: 2g; Carbs: 1g; Protein: 18g

LEMON CORNISH CHICKEN STUFFED WITH CRAB

Preparation Time:
30 minutes
(additional 2-3 hours marinade)

Cooking time:
1 hour 30 minutes

Servings:
2-4

INGREDIENTS:

- 2 Cornish chickens (about 13/4 pound each)
- Half lemon, half
- 4 Tbsp. western rub or poultry rub
- 2 cups stuffed with crab meat

DIRECTIONS:

1. Rinse chicken thoroughly inside and outside, tap lightly and let it dry.
2. Roast the chicken at 375 ° F until the inside temperature of the thickest part of the chicken breast reaches 170 ° F, the thigh reaches 180 ° F, and the juice is clear.
3. Test the crab meat stuffing to see if the temperature has reached 165 ° F.
4. Place the roasted chicken under a loose foil tent for 15 minutes before serving.

NUTRITION: Calories: 275, Carbs: 0g, Fat: 3g, Protein: 32g

TEQUILA LIME ROASTED TURKEY

Preparation Time: 10 minutes	**Cooking time:** 15 minutes	**Servings:** 3

INGREDIENTS:

- 9 garlic cloves
- 1 bone-in whole turkey (roughly 15 pounds), thawed
- 3 jalapño chills, cut in half & seeded
- 1 1/4 cups gold tequila
- 3 ounces olive oil
- 1 1/2 teaspoons pepper
- 3 limes cut into wedges
- 1 1/4 cups lime juice, fresh
- 3/4 cups each of orange juice & chicken broth
- 3 tablespoon chili powder
- 1 tablespoon salt

DIRECTIONS:

1. Take the turkey breast in a roasting pan, preferably pores and skin aspect up.
2. Place the jalapeno & garlic in a mini meals processor. Cover & process on high strength until chopped finely. Add the chili powder observed by using three-ounce. Of tequila, three-ounce. Of lime juice, oil, pepper, and salt. Cover & method on high electricity again till the aggregate is completely smooth.
3. Next, use a spoon or fingers; to loosen the turkey pores and skin & rub the organized garlic aggregate over and underneath the turkey pores and skin. Calmly pour the leftover blend on top of the turkey. Make sure that it doesn't touch the bone.
4. Pour the broth and orange juice observed using the leftover lime juice and tequila into a roasting pan.
5. Roast until the thermometer displays an analysis of 165 F, uncovered.
6. Place the turkey on a warm platter and then cover with aluminum foil. Let stand for 12 to 15 minutes before carving.
7. Spoon the pan juices on the turkey's pinnacle & garnish your dish with some clean lime wedges.
8. Enjoy.

NUTRITION: Calories: 94; Fat: 2g; Carbs: 1g; Protein: 18g

EASY RAPID-FIRE ROAST CHICKEN

Preparation Time:
10 minutes

Cooking time:
1 hour 30 minutes

Servings:
3 to 4

INGREDIENTS:

- 1 (4-pound) whole chicken, giblets removed
- Extra-virgin olive oil for rubbing
- 3 tablespoons Greek seasoning
- Juice of 1 lemon
- Butcher's string

DIRECTIONS:

1. Preheat your Griddle to 450°F.
2. Rub the bird generously all over with oil, including inside the cavity.
3. Put the chicken directly on the griddle top, breast-side up, and roast.
4. Let the meat rest for 10 minutes before carving.

NUTRITION: Calories: 229, Carbs: 0g, Fat: 15g, Protein: 23g

TURKEY LEGS

Preparation Time:
10 minutes

Cooking time:
5 hours

Servings:
4

INGREDIENTS:

- 4 turkey legs
- For the Brine:
- 1/2 cup curing salt
- 1 tablespoon whole black peppercorns
- 1 cup BBQ rub
- 1/2 cup brown sugar
- 2 bay leaves
- 2 teaspoons liquid smoke
- 16 cups of warm water
- 4 cups ice
- 8 cups of cold water

DIRECTIONS:

1. Bring the brine to a boil by pouring warm water into a large stockpot, adding peppercorn, bay leaves, liquid smoke, salt, sugar, and BBQ rub, and bringing it to a boil.
2. Pour cold water into the pot, add ice cubes and let the brine cool in the refrigerator. Remove the pot from the heat and bring it to room temperature.
3. Add the turkey legs to it, submerge them completely in it, and let them soak for 24 hours in the refrigerator.
4. Using paper towels, pat dry the turkey legs after 24 hours of bringing.
5. Cook the turkey on a hot griddle top until nicely browned and the internal temperature reaches 165 degrees F. Serve immediately.

NUTRITION: Calories: 416; Fat: 13.3 g; Carbs: 0 g; Protein: 69.8 g

SPICY CHICKEN BREASTS

Preparation Time: 45 minutes	**Cooking time:** 15 minutes	**Servings:** 4

INGREDIENTS:

- 4 chicken breasts, skinless & boneless.
- 1 tbsp. Red pepper flakes
- 1 tbsp. Chili powder
- 6 tbsp. Brown sugar
- 6 tbsp. BBQ sauce
- 1 cup. Pineapple juice

DIRECTIONS:

1. Seal the zip-lock bag with the chicken breasts. Sauce chicken breasts with the pineapple juice, BBQ sauce, brown sugar, chili powder, and red pepper flakes that you've combined in a separate bowl.
2. Place the Ziplock bag in the refrigerator overnight to keep the ingredients fresh.
3. Heat the griddle grill over medium-high heat until it sizzles. Marinated chicken breasts should be cooked for 12-15 minutes, depending on how you want your chicken.
4. Serve.

NUTRITION: Calories: 255kcal, Protein: 35g, Carbs: 42g, Fat: 35g.

BUFFALO CHICKEN WINGS

Preparation Time:
10 minutes

Cooking time:
20 minutes

Servings:
8

INGREDIENTS:

- 1 Tbsp. sea salt
- 1 Tsp. ground black pepper
- ½ Tsp. garlic powder
- 4 Lbs. chicken wings
- 2 Tbsp. unsalted butter
- 1/3 cup buffalo sauce, like Moore's
- 1 tbsp. apple cider vinegar
- 1 tbsp. honey

DIRECTIONS:

1. Whisk the salt, pepper, and garlic powder in a large mixing basin. Toss the wings in the seasoning mixture to coat them entirely with it.
2. Turn on a griddle over medium heat and let it heat up.
3. Place the wings on the gridiron, ensuring they touch each other to ensure that the flesh remains moist on the bone while griddling occurs. Every 5 minutes, flip the wings over for a total of 20 minutes of cooking time. In a small saucepan, boil the butter, buffalo sauce, vinegar, and honey over low heat, constantly stirring until thoroughly combined. Combine the wings with the sauce in a large mixing bowl until well coated.
4. Cook the wings for one to two minutes on each side of the Griddle or until the skin is crisp. Return the wings to the dish with the sauce and toss to combine before serving.

NUTRITION: Calories: 764, Fat: 55g, Carbohydrates: 2g, Protein: 63g

CLASSIC BBQ CHICKEN

Preparation Time: 5 minutes	**Cooking time:** 1 hour 45 minutes	**Servings:** 6

INGREDIENTS:

- 3 pounds of your favorite chicken, including legs, thighs, wings, and breasts, skin-on
- Salt
- 1 tsp. Olive oil
- ½ Cup barbecue sauce, like Hickory
- Mesquite or homemade

DIRECTIONS:

1. Olive oil and salt are applied to the chicken breasts. Preheat the skillet to a high heat setting before you begin. Cook the chicken skin side down for 5-10 minutes on the grill until it becomes crispy.
2. Cook the skillet for 30 minutes at medium-low heat with an aluminum foil cover. Toss the chicken with the barbecue sauce and turn it over. Cook the chicken for 20 minutes under the second layer of aluminum foil.
3. Baste, cover, and cook for another 30 minutes, basting and rotating many times during this time. At 165°F and the juices are flowing clear indication that the chicken is ready to eat.
4. To finish, baste with more barbecue sauce and serve!.

NUTRITION: Calories: 764, Fat: 55g, Carbohydrates: 2g, Protein: 63g

ELK CHILI

 Preparation Time: 30 minutes

 Cooking time: 1 hour

 Servings: 6

INGREDIENTS:

- 1 1/2 pounds of ground elk meat
- Two large yellow onions, diced
- 2 (10 oz) cans of tomato sauce
- 1 (14.5 oz) can Italian-style stewed tomatoes
- 1 (15 oz) can kidney beans, drained
- 1 (4 oz) can dice green chiles (optional)
- 1 1/2 tsp chili powder
- 1 1/2 teaspoons ground cumin
- 1 tsp dried oregano
- 1 tsp salt
- 1 tsp black pepper
- 1/2 cup brown sugar

DIRECTIONS:

1. Cook the ground elk with all the onion in a large deep skillet until evenly dispersed over moderate heat.
2. Drain off excess grease.
3. Pour the tomato sauce, stewed tomatoes, kidney beans, and green chilies into the skillet with the beef, and stir to combine.
4. Season with chili powder, cumin, pepper, salt, oregano, and brown sugar levels.
5. While covered, ook at a low temperature for a minimum of 1 hour.

NUTRITION: Calories: 307, Fat: 2.4 g, Cholesterol: 52 mg, Carb: 45.2-g, Protein: 28.1 g

LAMB

SPICY CHINESE CUMIN LAMB SKEWERS

Preparation Time: 20 minutes	**Cooking time:** 10 minutes	**Servings:** 10

INGREDIENTS:

- Lb. lamb shoulder, cut into 1/2-inch pieces
- 10 skewers
- Tbsp. ground cumin
- Tbsp. red pepper flakes
- 1 Tbsp. salt

DIRECTIONS:

1. Thread the lamb pieces onto skewers.
2. Preheat your Griddle at medium-high temperature.
3. Coat the top of the Griddle using cooking spray.
4. Place the skewers on the hot griddle top and cook while turning occasionally. Sprinkle cumin, pepper flakes, and salt every time you turn the skewer.
5. Serve and enjoy.

NUTRITION: Calories: 77, Fat: 5g, Carbs: 2g, Protein: 6g

FLAVORS LAMB CHOPS

 Preparation Time: **15-30 minutes**

 Cooking time: **8 minutes**

 Servings: **6**

INGREDIENTS

- 6 lamb chops
- 2 tbsp. fresh mint, chopped
- 1/2 tsp. pepper
- 2 tbsp. olive oil
- 1/2 tsp. kosher salt

INSTRUCTIONS

1. Preheat the Griddle to a high heat setting before you begin. Season the lamb chops with pepper and salt after brushing them with oil. Cook the lamb chops for 5 minutes on a heated griddle top until they are cooked through.
2. After flipping the lamb chops, cook for another 3 minutes. Prepare the dish and serve it to your guests.

NUTRITION: Calories: 255kcal, Protein: 35g, Carbs: 42g, Fat: 35g.

GARLIC AND ROSEMARY LAMB CHOPS ON THE GRIDDLE

 Preparation Time: 20 minutes

 Cooking time: 12 minutes

 Servings: 4

INGREDIENTS:

- 2 lb. lamb loin, thick-cut
- 4 garlic cloves, minced
- Tbsp. rosemary leaves, fresh chopped
- 1 Tbsp. kosher salt
- 1/2 Tbsp. black pepper
- 1 lemon zest
- 1/4 cup olive oil

DIRECTIONS:

1. I combine the garlic, lemon zest, oil, salt, and black pepper in a small mixing bowl, then pour the mixture over the lamb. The lamb.
2. Make sure the lamb chops are evenly coated by flipping them over. Marinate the chops for an hour in the fridge.
3. Preheat your Griddle to high heat, then sear the lamb for 3 minutes on each side.
4. Reduce the heat & cook the chops for 6 minutes or until the internal temperature reaches 150°F.
5. Remove the lamb from the Griddle and wrap it in foil.
6. Before serving, let it rest for 5 minutes.
7. Enjoy!

NUTRITION: Calories: 171, Fat: 8g, Carbs: 1g, Protein: 23g

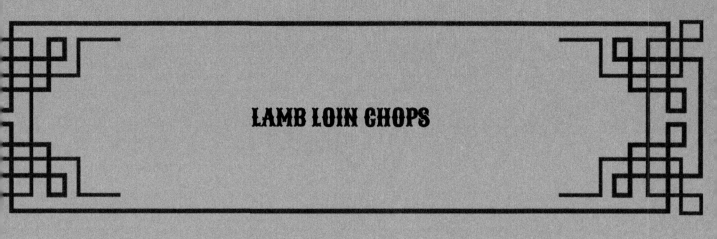

LAMB LOIN CHOPS

Preparation Time:
10 minutes

Cooking time:
10 minutes

Servings:
6

INGREDIENTS:

- 2 Tbsp. herbs de Provence
- 1-1/2 Tbsp. olive oil
- 2 garlic cloves, minced
- 2 Tbsp. lemon juice
- 5-ounce lamb loin chops
- Salt and black pepper to taste

DIRECTIONS:

1. In a small mixing bowl, mix herbs de Provence, oil, garlic, and juice. Rub the mixture on the lamb chops, then refrigerate for an hour.
2. Preheat your Griddle to medium-high, then lightly oil the griddle top.
3. Put salt and black pepper into the lamb chops. Arrange them onto the griddle top and cook for about 4-6 minutes per side.
4. Place the chops on an aluminum-covered plate after removing them from the heat. Let rest for 5 minutes before serving.

NUTRITION: Calories: 570, Fat: 44g, Carbs: 1g, Protein: 42g

SIMPLE LAMB CHOPS

Preparation Time:
10 minutes

Cooking time:
12 minutes

Servings:
6

INGREDIENTS:

- 6 (6-ounce) lamb chops
- 3 tablespoons olive oil
- Salt and ground black pepper, as required

DIRECTIONS:

1. Preheat the Griddle to 450 degrees F.
2. Put some oil into the lamb chops and season with salt and black pepper evenly.
3. Arrange the chops onto the griddle top and cook for about 4-6 minutes per side.
4. Serve the chops hot after removing them from the heat.

NUTRITION: Calories 376, Total Fat 19.5 g, Cholesterol 153 mg, Sodium 156 mg, Fiber 0 g, Sugar 0 g, Protein 47.8 g

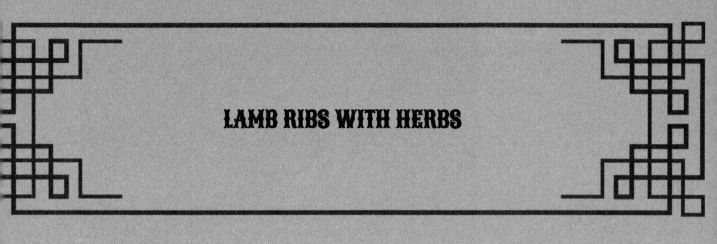

LAMB RIBS WITH HERBS

Preparation Time:
15 minutes

Cooking time:
2 hours

Servings:
6

INGREDIENTS:

- 4 Racks of Raider Red Lamb Riblets
- For the marinade:
- 1/2 Cup of olive oil
- 4 Juiced large lemons
- And 1/2 cups of smoked garlic cloves
- Tbsp. of dry Chinese mustard
- Tbsp. of dried Tarragon
- 2 Tbsp. of Date Night Heat seasoning

DIRECTIONS:

1. Combine the marinade in your food processor and mix all the ingredients until you get a liquefied mixture.
2. Score the lamb ribs in the shape of a diamond cut to allow the fats to render some of it and let the marinade penetrate the lamb ribs.
3. Place the ribs in a large plastic container or in an extra-large freezer bag; then pour the marinade on top. Refrigerate for about 48 hours.
4. Once ready to cook your meat, preheat your Griddle to a temperature of about 250°F.
5. When the Griddle is hot, place the ribs with the bone side down for about 3 hours.
6. Spoon the prepared marinade right on top of the ribs to create a friendly and crusty topping.
7. When the ribs of lamb reach an internal temperature of about 190°F, pull off the lamb ribs and cover; then let rest for about 5 to 10 minutes.
8. For about 5-10 minutes, let the meat rest, then serve and enjoy your dish!

NUTRITION: Calories: 265, Fat: 13g, Carbohydrates: 10g, Protein: 26g

HERBED RACK OF LAMB

Preparation Time:
15 minutes

Cooking time:
2 hours

Servings:
3

INGREDIENTS:

- 2 tablespoons fresh sage
- 2 tablespoons fresh rosemary
- 2 tablespoons fresh thyme
- 2 garlic cloves, peeled
- 1 tablespoon honey
- Salt and ground black pepper, as required
- 1/4 cup olive oil
- 1 (1 1/2-pound) rack of lamb, trimmed

DIRECTIONS:

1. In your food processor, add all ingredients except for oil and rack of lamb rack and pulse until well combined.
2. As the motor runs, slowly add the oil and pulse until smooth paste forms.
3. Coat the rib rack with paste generously and refrigerate for about 2 hours.
4. Preheat your gas griddle to 225 degrees F.
5. Arrange the rack of lamb onto the griddle top and cook for about 2 hours.
6. Remove the rack of lamb from the heat and place it on a cutting board for about 10-15 minutes before slicing.
7. W/ a sharp knife, cut the rack into individual ribs and serve.

NUTRITION: Calories 566, Fat 37.5 g, Cholest 151 mg, Sodium 214 mg, Carbs 9.8 g, Fiber 2.2 g, Sugar 5.8g, Protein 46.7 g

CLASSIC ROSEMARY LAMB

Preparation Time: 20 minutes

Cooking time: 3 hours 15 minutes

Servings: 2

INGREDIENTS:

- Rack lamb, rib
- A bunch of fresh asparagus
- Rosemary, springs
- 1 drunken baby potato
- Tablespoons olive oil
- Pepper and salt to taste
- 1/2 cup butter

DIRECTIONS:

1. Preheat your Griddle to 225°F in advance.
2. Get rid of the membrane from the ribs' backside and then drizzle on both sides with olive oil; finally, sprinkle with the rosemary. Combine the butter with potatoes in a deep baking dish.
3. Place the rack of prepared ribs alongside the dish of potatoes on the grates. For 3 hours, cook the meat until it reaches 145°F.
4. During the last 15 minutes of cooking, don't forget to add asparagus to the potatoes and continue to cook until it turns tender. Slice the lamb into desired pieces and serve with cooked asparagus and potatoes.

NUTRITION: Calories: 660, Fat: 57g, Cholesterol: 150mg, Carbs: 17g, Protein: 20g

COLA FLAVORED RACK OF LAMB

Preparation Time: 15 minutes	**Cooking time:** 3 hours	**Servings:** 12

INGREDIENTS:

- 4 (11/2-pound) racks of lamb, trimmed
- 1 tablespoon unsweetened cocoa powder
- 1 tablespoon brown sugar
- 1 tablespoon smoked paprika
- Salt and ground black pepper, as required
- 1 cup cherry cola

DIRECTIONS:

1. Preheat your gas griddle to 225 degrees F.
2. With a sharp knife, make 1/2x1/4-inch cuts in each rack of lamb.
3. In a bowl, place the remaining ingredients except for cherry cola and mix until well combined.
4. Rub the racks with sugar mixture generously.
5. Arrange the racks onto the griddle top and cook for about 2-3 hours, coating with cherry cola after every 1 hour.
6. Remove the racks from the fire and place them onto a cutting board for about 10-15 minutes before slicing.
7. Use a knife and cut each rack of lamb into individual ribs and serve.

NUTRITION: Calories 437, Fat 16.8g, Cholesterol 204 mg, Sodium 186 mg, Carbs 3.6g, Fiber 0.4 g, Sugar 2.7g, Protein 63.9 g

WINE FLAVORED LEG OF LAMB

 Preparation Time: 15 minutes

 Cooking time: 5 hours

 Servings: 8

INGREDIENTS:

- 1/2 cup olive oil
- 1/2 cup red wine vinegar
- 1/2 cup dry white wine
- 1 tablespoon garlic, minced
- 1 teaspoon dried marjoram, crushed
- 1 teaspoon dried rosemary, crushed
- Salt and ground black pepper, as required
- 1 (5-pound) leg of lamb

DIRECTIONS:

1. Combine all ingredients except for the leg of lamb in a bowl and mix well.
2. Add marinade and leg of lamb in a large bag with resalable.
3. Seal the bag and shake to coat thoroughly.
4. Refrigerate for about 4-6 hours, flipping occasionally.
5. Preheat the Griddle to 225 degrees F.
6. Arrange the leg of lamb onto the griddle surface and cook for about 4-5 hours.
7. Remove the leg of lamb from the fire and place it on a cutting board for about 20 minutes before slicing.
8. Use a knife and cut the leg of lamb into desired-sized slices and serve.

NUTRITION: Calories 653, Fat 33.4g, Cholesterol 255mg, Sodium 237mg, Carbs 1g, Fiber 0.1g, Sugar 0.2g, Protein 79.7g

SWEET & TANGY BRAISED LAMB SHANK

Preparation Time:
15 minutes

Cooking time:
8-10 hours

Servings:
2

INGREDIENTS:

- 2 (1 1/4-pound) lamb shanks
- 1-2 cups of water
- 1/4 cup brown sugar
- 1/3 cup rice wine
- 1/3 cup soy sauce
- 1 tablespoon dark sesame oil
- 4 (1 1/2x1/2-inch) orange zest strips
- 2 (3-inch long) cinnamon sticks
- 1 1/2 teaspoons Chinese five-spice powder

DIRECTIONS:

1. Preheat your Griddle to 225-250 degrees F.
2. Pierce each lamb shank several times with a sharp knife.
3. Add all remaining ingredients to a bowl and mix until sugar is dissolved.
4. Spread the sugar mixture evenly over the lamb shanks in a large foil pan.
5. Griddle the foil pan for about 8-10 hours, flipping it after every 30 minutes. (Add enough water to keep the liquid 1/2 inch above the surface if necessary).
6. Remove from the heat and serve hot.

NUTRITION: Calories 1200, Fat 48.4g, Cholesterol 510mg, Sodium 2000mg, Carbs 39.7g, Fiber 0.3g, Sugar 29g, Protein 161.9g

HAPPY SHRIMP

Preparation Time:
5 minutes

Cooking time:
4 minutes

Servings:
4

INGREDIENTS:

- Jumbo shrimp peeled and cleaned - 1 lb.
- Oil - 2 Tbsp.
- Salt - 1/2 Tbsp.
- Skewers - 4-5
- Pepper – 1/8 Tbsp.
- Garlic salt - 1/2 Tbsp.

DIRECTIONS:

1. Preheat the Griddle to 375 degrees.
2. In a bowl, combine all the ingredients.
3. After washing and drying the shrimp, mix it well with the oil and seasonings.
4. Add skewers to the shrimp and set the bowl of shrimp aside.
5. Open the skewers and flip them.
6. Cook for 4 more minutes. Remove when the shrimp is opaque and pink.

NUTRITION: Carbohydrates: 1.3 g, Protein: 19 g, Fat: 1.4 g, Sodium: 805 mg, Cholesterol: 179 mg

LOBSTER TAILS

 Preparation Time: 10 minutes

 Cooking time: 35 minutes

 Servings: 4

INGREDIENTS:

- 2 lobster tails, each about 10 ounces
- For the Sauce:
- 2 tablespoons chopped parsley
- 1/4 teaspoon garlic salt
- 1 teaspoon paprika
- 1/4 teaspoon ground black pepper
- 1/4 teaspoon old bay seasoning
- 8 tablespoons butter, unsalted
- 2 tablespoons lemon juice

DIRECTIONS:

1. Preheat the Griddle to 250 degrees
2. Prepare the lobster and for this, cut the shell from the middle to the tail by using kitchen shears and then take the meat from the shell, keeping it attached to the base of the crab tail.
3. Butterfly the crab meat by making a slit down the middle, place lobster tails on a baking sheet, pour 1 tablespoon of sauce over each lobster tail, and reserve the remaining sauce.
4. When the Griddle has preheated, place crab tails on the griddle top, and shut the cook for 30 minutes until opaque. When done, transfer lobster tails to a dish and then serve with the remaining sauce.

NUTRITION: Calories: 290, Fat: 22 g, Carbs: 1 g, Protein: 20 g

JERK SHRIMP

Preparation Time:
15 minutes

Cooking time:
0 minutes

Servings:
6

INGREDIENTS:

- 2 pounds shrimp, peeled, deveined
- 3 tablespoons olive oil
- 1 teaspoon garlic powder
- 1 teaspoon of sea salt
- 1/4 teaspoon ground cayenne
- 1 tablespoon brown sugar
- 1/8 teaspoon smoked paprika
- 1 tablespoon smoked paprika
- 1/4 teaspoon ground thyme
- 1 lime, zester

DIRECTIONS:

1. Preheat the Griddle to 250 degrees.
2. Meanwhile, prepare the spice mix; take a small bowl, place all of its ingredients, and stir until mixed.
3. Put shrimp in a large bowl, sprinkle with spice mix, drizzle with oil, and toss until well coated.
4. When the Griddle has preheated, place shrimps on the griddle top, and shut the cook for 3 minutes per side until firm and thoroughly cooked.
5. Transfer the shrimps to a dish and serve.

NUTRITION: Calories: 131, Fat: 4.3 g, Carbs: 0 g, Protein: 22 g, Fiber: 0 g

CITRUS SALMON

Preparation Time:
15 minutes

Cooking time:
30 minutes

Servings:
6

INGREDIENTS:

- 2 (1-lb.) salmon fillets
- Salt & freshly ground black pepper to taste
- 1 Tbsp. seafood seasoning
- 2 lemons, sliced
- 2 limes, sliced

DIRECTIONS:

1. Set the griddle temperature to 225 degrees F and preheat for 15 minutes.
2. Evenly season the salmon fillets with salt, black pepper, and seafood seasoning.
3. Place the salmon fillets on Griddle and top each with lemon and lime slices evenly.
4. Cook for about 30 minutes.
5. Take the salmon fillets off the heat and serve them hot.

NUTRITION: Calories: 327, Carbohydrates: 1g, Protein: 36.1g, Fat: 19.8g, Sugar: 0.2g, Sodium: 237mg, Fiber: 0.

OMEGA-3 RICH SALMON

 Preparation Time: 15 minutes

 Cooking time: 20 minutes

 Servings: 4

INGREDIENTS:

- 6 (6-ounce.) skinless salmon fillets
- 1/3 C. olive oil
- 1/4 C. spice rubs
- 1/4 C. honey
- 2 Tbsp. Sriracha
- 2 Tbsp. fresh lime juice

DIRECTIONS:

1. Set the griddle temperature to 300 degrees F and preheat for 15 minutes.
2. Coat salmon fillets w/ olive oil and season with rub evenly.
3. Stir the remaining ingredients in a small bowl.
4. Arrange salmon fillets onto the Griddle, flat-side up and cook for about 7-10 minutes per side, coating with the honey mixture once halfway through.
5. Serve hot alongside the remaining honey mixture.

NUTRITION: Calories: 384, Carbohydrates: 15.7g, Protein: 33g, Fat: 21.7g, Sugar: 11.6g, Sodium: 621mg, Fiber: 0g

ENTICING MAHI-MAHI

 Preparation Time: 10 minutes

 Cooking time: 10 minutes

 Servings: 4

INGREDIENTS:

- 4 (6-ounce.) mahi-mahi fillets
- 2 Tbsp. olive oil
- Salt & freshly ground black pepper to taste

INSTRUCTIONS:

1. Set the griddle temperature to 350 F and preheat for 15 minutes.
2. Coat fish fillets w/ olive oil and season with salt and black pepper evenly.
3. Place the fish fillets onto the griddle top and cook for about 5 minutes per side.
4. Remove the fish fillets from the heat and serve hot.

NUTRITION: Calories: 195, Carbohydrates: 0g, Protein: 31.6g, Fat: 7g, Sugar: 0g, Sodium: 182mg, Fiber: 0g

BLACKENED CATFISH

Preparation Time:
10 minutes

Cooking time:
10 minutes

Servings:
4

INGREDIENTS:

Spice blend
- 1 teaspoon granulated garlic
- 1/4 teaspoon cayenne pepper
- 1/2 cup Cajun seasoning
- 1 teaspoon ground thyme
- 1 teaspoon ground oregano
- 1 teaspoon onion powder
- 1 tablespoon smoked paprika
- 1 teaspoon pepper

Fish
- 4 catfish fillets
- Salt to taste
- 1/2 cup butter

INSTRUCTIONS:

1. In a bowl, mix the ingredients for the spice blend.
2. Salt and spice the fish on both sides.
3. Set your gas griddle to 450 degrees F.
4. Heat your Griddle at medium temperature, add the butter, then add the fillets.
5. Cook for 5 minutes per side.

NUTRITION: Calories: 283, Carbs: 1g, Fat: 19g, Protein: 27g

SWORDFISH STEAKS WITH CORN SALSA

Preparation Time:
10 minutes

Cooking time:
15 minutes

Servings:
4

INGREDIENTS:

- 4 whole ears of corn, husked
- Olive oil, as needed
- Salt and black pepper to taste
- 1-pint cherry tomatoes
- 1 whole Serrano chili, chopped
- 1 whole red onion, diced
- 1 whole lime, juiced
- 4 whole swordfish fillets

INSTRUCTIONS:

1. When ready to cook, set the Griddle to High and preheat for 15 minutes.
2. Place the corn on the griddle top and cook for 12 to 15 minutes, or until cooked through and lightly browned. Set aside to cool.
3. Transfer to a medium bowl. Stir in the tomatoes, Serrano, red onion, and lime juice.
4. Arrange the fillets on the griddle top and cook for about 18 minutes.
5. Serve the swordfish topped with corn salsa.

NUTRITION Calories: 87, Carbs: 10g, Fat: 2g, Protein: 6g

FISH TACOS

Preparation Time:
10 minutes

Cooking time:
8 minutes

Servings:
12

INGREDIENTS

- 1/4 teaspoon cayenne pepper
- 1/2 teaspoon cumin
- 1 1/2 teaspoon paprika
- 1 teaspoon garlic powder
- 1 teaspoon dried oregano
- Salt and pepper to taste
- 1 1/2 lb. codfish
- 12 tortillas
- Salsa
- Avocado, sliced
- Sour cream

INSTRUCTIONS

1. Preheat your Griddle to 350 degrees F.
2. Combine the salt, pepper, herbs, and spices. Whisk this mixture on the fish.
3. Cook the fish for 4 minutes per side.
4. Shred the fish with a fork. Place on top of the tortillas. Top with salsa, sour cream, and avocado.
5. Roll up the tortillas and serve.

NUTRITION: Calories: 117, Carbs: 2g, Fat: 6g, Protein: 12g

VEGETABLE

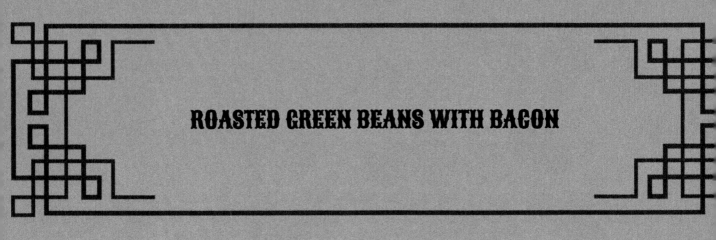

ROASTED GREEN BEANS WITH BACON

Preparation Time: 15 minutes

Cooking time: 20 minutes

Servings: 4/6

INGREDIENTS

- 1-pound green beans
- 4 strips of bacon, cut into small pieces
- 4 tablespoons extra virgin olive oil
- 2 cloves garlic, minced
- 1 teaspoon salt

INSTRUCTIONS

1. Fire the Griddle to 400F and let it preheat for at most 15 minutes
2. Spread out all ingredients evenly on a sheet tray.
3. Place the tray on the griddle top and cook for 20 minutes.

NUTRITION Calories: 65 Cal, Fat: 5.3 g, Carbohydrates: 3 g, Protein: 1.3 g, Fiber: 0 g

GRILLED CORN WITH HONEY BUTTER

Preparation Time: 15 minutes	**Cooking time:** 10 minutes	**Servings:** 4/6

INGREDIENTS

- 6 pieces of corn, husked
- 2 tablespoons olive oil
- Salt and pepper to taste
- 1/2 cup butter, room temperature
- 1/2 cup honey

INSTRUCTIONS

1. Fire the Griddle to 350F.
2. Coat corn with oil and add salt and pepper
3. Place the corn on the griddle top and cook for 10 minutes. For even cooking, flip the corn halfway through the cooking time.
4. Meanwhile, mix the butter and honey in a small bowl. Set aside.
5. Remove corn from heat and coat with honey butter sauce

NUTRITION: Calories: 387, Cal Fat: 21.6 g, Carbohydrates: 51.2 g, Protein: 5 g, Fiber: 0 g

APPLE VEGGIE BURGER

 Preparation Time: 10 minutes

 Cooking time: 40 minutes

 Servings: 4/6

INGREDIENTS

- 3 Tbsp. ground flax or ground chia
- 1/3 cup of warm water
- 1/2 cup rolled oats
- 1 cup chickpeas, drained and rinsed
- 1 Tsp. cumin
- 1/2 cup onion
- 1 Tsp. dried basil
- 2 granny smith apples
- 1/3 cup parsley or cilantro, chopped
- 2 Tbsp. soy sauce
- 2 Tsp. liquid smoke
- 2 cloves garlic, minced
- 1 Tsp. chili powder
- 1/4 Tsp. black pepper

INSTRUCTIONS

1. Preheat the Griddle to 225°F.
2. In a separate bowl, add chickpeas and mash. Whisk together the ingredients along with the dipped flax seeds.
3. Form patties from this mixture.
4. Put the patties on the rack of the Griddle and cook them for 20 minutes on each side.
5. When brown, take them out and serve.

NUTRITION Calories: 241, Cal Fat: 5 g, Carbohydrates: 40 g, Protein: 9 g, Fiber: 10.3 g

ZUCCHINI WITH RED POTATOES

Preparation Time:
15 minutes

Cooking time:
20 minutes

Servings:
4/6

INGREDIENTS

- 2 zucchinis, sliced in 3/4-inch-thick disks
- 1 red pepper, cut into strips
- 2 yellow squashes, sliced into 3/4-inch-thick disks
- 1 medium red onion, cut into wedges
- 6 small red potatoes cut into chunks
- 1 cup extra virgin olive oil
- 1 teaspoon salt
- 1 cup balsamic vinegar
- 2 Tsp. Dijon mustard
- 1 teaspoon pepper

INSTRUCTIONS

1. Make a vinaigrette by blending olive oil, Dijon mustard, salt, pepper, and balsamic vinegar in a medium bowl.
2. Set all the veggies and pour the vinaigrette mixture over it and evenly toss.
3. Put the vegetable on a griddle top and then cook for 20 minutes at medium heat.
4. Serve and enjoy the food.

NUTRITION: Calories: 381, Cal Fat: 17.6 g, Carbohydrates: 49 g, Protein: 6.7 g, Fiber: 6.5 g

COCONUT BACON

Preparation Time:
10 minutes

Cooking time:
30 minutes

Servings:
4/6

INGREDIENTS

- 3 1/2 cups flaked coconut
- 1 Tbsp. pure maple syrup
- 1 Tbsp. water
- 2 Tbsp. liquid smoke
- 1 Tbsp. soy sauce
- 1 Tsp. smoked paprika (optional)

INSTRUCTIONS

1. Preheat the Griddle to 325°F.
2. Stir liquid smoke, maple syrup, soy sauce, and water together in a large bowl.
3. Pour flaked coconut over the mixture. Add it to a cooking sheet.
4. Place on top of the Griddle.
5. Cook it for 30 minutes, and every 7-8 minutes, keep flipping the sides.
6. Serve and enjoy.

NUTRITION: Calories: 1244, Cal Fat: 100 g, Carbohydrates: 70 g, Protein: 16 g, Fiber: 2 g

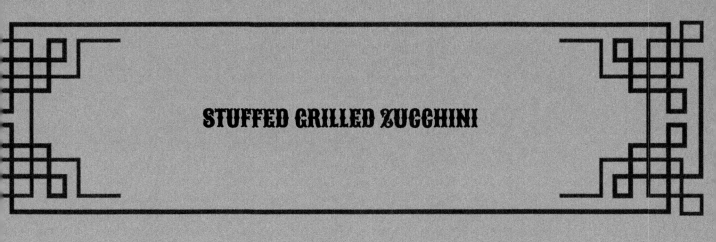

STUFFED GRILLED ZUCCHINI

Preparation Time:
15 minutes

Cooking time:
10 minutes

Servings:
6

INGREDIENTS

- 4 zucchini medium
- 5 Tbsp. olive oil, divided
- 2 Tbsp. red onion, finely chopped
- 1/4 Tbsp. garlic, minced
- 1/2 cup breadcrumbs, dry
- 1/2 cup shredded mozzarella cheese, part-skim
- 1/2 Tbsp. salt
- 1 Tbsp. fresh mint, minced
- 3 Tbsp. parmesan cheese, grated

INSTRUCTIONS

1. Halve zucchini lengthwise and scoop the pulp out. Leave 1/4 -inch shell. Now brush using 2 Tbsp oil, set aside, and chop the pulp.
2. Saute onion and pulp in a skillet, large, then add garlic and cook for about 1 minute.
3. Add breadcrumbs and cook while stirring for about 2 minutes until golden brown.
4. Add the mozzarella cheese, salt, and mint after removing everything from the heat. Fill the zucchini shells with the cheese mixture and sprinkle with parmesan.
5. Turn your Griddle on to 375°F.
6. Place stuffed zucchini on the griddle top and cook while covered for about 8-10 minutes until tender.
7. Serve warm and enjoy.

NUTRITION: Calories: 214, Cal Fat: 12 g, Carbohydrates: 42 g, Protein: 27 g, Fiber: 17 g

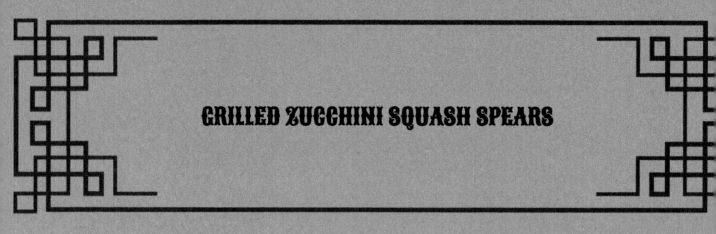

GRILLED ZUCCHINI SQUASH SPEARS

Preparation Time:
5 minutes

Cooking time:
10 minutes

Servings:
4

INGREDIENTS

- 4 zucchini medium
- 2 Tbsp. olive oil
- 1 Tbsp. sherry vinegar
- 2 thyme leaves pulled
- Salt to taste
- Pepper to taste

INSTRUCTIONS

1. Wash zucchini, cut off ends, then cut lengthwise in half, then into thirds.
2. In a medium zip lock bag, place all the other ingredients, and then add spears.
3. Coat the zucchini well by tossing well and mixing.
4. For about 15 minutes, preheat the Griddle to 350°F.
5. Put the spears directly on the griddle top with the cut side facing up after removing them from the zip lock bag.
6. Cook until zucchini is tender.
7. Remove them from the heat and enjoy.

NUTRITION Calories 93, Total fat 7.4g, Saturated fat 1.1g, Total carbs 7.1g, Protein 2.4g,

GRILLED ASPARAGUS & HONEY-GLAZED CARROTS

 Preparation Time: 15 minutes

 Cooking time: 35 minutes

 Servings: 4

INGREDIENTS

- 1 bunch asparagus, woody ends removed
- 2 Tbsp. olive oil
- 1 lb. peeled carrots
- 2 Tbsp. honey
- Sea salt to taste
- Lemon zest to taste

INSTRUCTIONS

1. Under cold water, rinse the vegetables.
2. Add generous amounts of oil and salt to the asparagus.
3. Sprinkle carrots lightly with salt and generously drizzle with honey.
4. For about 15 minutes, preheat your Griddle to 350°F.
5. Place the carrots first on the griddle top and cook for about 10-15 minutes.
6. Now place asparagus on the Griddle and cook both for about 15-20 minutes or until done to your liking.
7. Top with lemon zest, and enjoy.

NUTRITION: Calories 184, Total fat 7.3g, Saturated fat 1.1g, Protein 6g

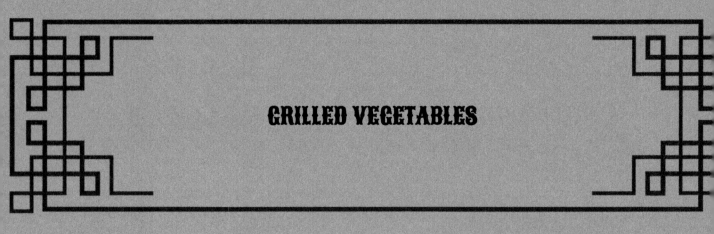

GRILLED VEGETABLES

Preparation Time:
5 minutes

Cooking time:
15 minutes

Servings:
5

INGREDIENTS

- 1 veggie tray
- 1/4 cup vegetable oil
- 1-2 Tbsp. Trigger veggie seasoning

INSTRUCTIONS

1. Preheat your Griddle to 375°F.
2. With the oil and seasoning, toss the vegetables on a large sheet pan.
3. Place on the griddle top and cook for about 10-15 minutes.
4. Remove, serve, and enjoy.

NUTRITION Calories 44, Fat 5g, Saturated fat 0g, Protein 0g

MASHED POTATOES

 Preparation Time: 5 minutes

 Cooking time: 40 minutes

 Servings: 12

INGREDIENTS

- 5 lbs. Yukon gold potatoes, large dice
- 1 1/2 sticks butter, softened
- 1 1/2 cup cream, room temperature
- Kosher salt, to taste
- White pepper, to taste

INSTRUCTIONS

1. When ready to cook, set the temperature to 300°F and preheat for 15 minutes
2. Strip and dice potatoes into 1/2" cubes.
3. Place the potatoes in a foil tin and cover. Roast in the Griddle until tender (about 40 minutes).
4. Put together combine cream and butter until it dissolved.
5. Mash potatoes using a potato masher. Gradually add in the cream and butter mixture, and mix using the masher. Be careful not to overwork, or the potatoes will become gluey.
6. Season with salt and pepper to taste. Enjoy!

NUTRITION Calories: 230Protein: 9g , Fat: 2g, Carbs: 45g

Conclusion

There are so many types of gas griddles on the market that it's easy to choose one that's right for you. Before buying one, you should think about its size and what type of cooking you will do with it. Most people prefer non-stick griddles because they are easy to clean and maintain. This type of gas griddle is beneficial when you want to prepare different types of foods, like meat, fish, chicken, and others.

The recipes you can prepare on your gas griddle are awe-inspiring, and they will make you feel that your investment was worth it. Be careful when buying one so that you don't end up with a gas griddle that will not fulfill all your expectations and needs.

When looking for the best outdoor gas griddle, you need to consider the amount of money you want to spend. When choosing the right one, it's also important to consider the type of material used in its construction.

Follow the tips discussed and choose the best gas griddle for your home and needs because it will help you cook different types of food without any problems.

I hope the recipes in this book will give you many options for cooking. They are delicious and will make the house smells delicious. They can be prepared quickly and easily, which means you won't spend too much time in the kitchen.

Appendix A:

Measurement Conversions

Volume Equivalents (Liquid)

US STANDARD	US STANDARD (OUNCES)	METRIC (APPROXIMATE)
2 tablespoons	1 fl. oz.	30 mL
1/4 cup	2 fl. oz.	60 mL
1/2 cup	4 fl. oz.	120 mL
1 cup	8 fl. oz.	240 mL
1 1/2 cups	12 fl. oz.	355 mL
2 cups or 1 pint	16 fl. oz.	475 mL
4 cups or 1 quart	32 fl. oz.	1 L
1 gallon	128 fl. oz.	4 L

Volume Equivalents (Dry)

US STANDARD	METRIC (APPROXIMATE)
1/8 teaspoon	0.5 mL
1/4 teaspoon	1 mL
1/2 teaspoon	2 mL
3/4 teaspoon	4 mL
1 teaspoon	5 mL
1 tablespoon	15 mL
1/4 cup	59 mL
1/3 cup	79 mL
1/2 cup	118 mL
2/3 cup	156 mL
3/4 cup	177 mL
1 cup	235 mL
2 cups or 1 pint	475 mL
3 cups	700 mL
4 cups or 1 quart	1 L

Oven Temperatures

FAHRENHEIT	CELSIUS (APPROXIMATE)
250°F	120°C
300°F	150°C
325°F	165°C
350°F	180°C
375°F	190°C
400°F	200°C
425°F	220°C
450°F	230°C

Appendix 2:

Recipe Index

A

Apple Veggie Burger · 106

B

Baby Back Ribs · 40

Bacon and Venison Burgers · 25

Baked Venison Meatloaf · 59

Balsamic Vinegar Molasses Steak · 56

Basted Steak · 45

BBQ Spareribs with Mandarin Glaze · 43

Bean & Chile Burgers · 24

Beef Jerky · 61

Beef Tacos · 54

Best-Ever Cheddar Burgers · 20

Bison Tomahawk Steak · 58

Blackened Catfish · 100

Bourbon Glazed Turkey Legs · 68

Brunch Burger · 26

Buffalo Chicken Wings · 78

C

Cajun Chicken Breasts · 69

Cajun Chicken Rub · 37

Cheesesteak · 19

Cherry Smoked Strip Steak · 63

Chicken · 67

Chicken Kabobs with Vegetable · 66

Citrus Salmon · 97

Citrus-Brined Pork Roast · 41

Classic BBQ Chicken · 79

Classic Cajun Rub · 35

Classic Rosemary Lamb · 89

Coconut Bacon · 108

Coffee Meat Rub · 36

Cola Flavored Rack of Lamb · 90

Crunchy Chicken Burgers · 22

E

Easy Rapid-Fire Roast Chicken · 75

Elk Chili · 80

Enticing Mahi-Mahi · 99

F

Fish Tacos · 102

Flavors Lamb Chops · 83

French Toast Sticks · 14

G

Garlic and Rosemary Lamb Chops on the Griddle · 84

Grapefruit Juice Marinade · 33

Griddle Pancake · 13

Grilled Asparagus & Honey-Glazed Carrots · 111

Grilled Corn with Honey Butter · 105

Grilled Vegetables · 112

Grilled Zucchini Squash Spears · 110

H

Happy Shrimp · 94

Herbed Beef Eye Fillet · 55

Herbed Rack of Lamb · 88

Honey Cured Ham Ribs · 49

Honey Soy Pork Chops · 50

I
Italian Hamburgers · 21

J
Jerk Rub · 34

Jerk Shrimp · 96

L
Lamb Loin Chops · 85

Lamb Ribs with Herbs · 87

Lemon Cornish Chicken Stuffed with Crab · 73

Lobster Tails · 95

M
Mashed Potatoes · 113

Meaty Chuck Short Ribs · 64

Memphis Rub · 38

Montreal Steak Rub · 29

N
No-Fuss Tuna Burgers · 27

O
Omega-3 Rich Salmon · 98

P
Peanut Butter and Vanilla Toast · 17

Peruvian Chicken Marinade · 32

Pineapple Pork BBQ · 42

Pork Burnt Ends · 46

Pork Kebabs · 47

Pork Sausages · 44

Q
Quick Rosemary Garlic Rub · 30

R
Roasted Green Beans with Bacon · 104

Rosemary Dijon Pork Chops · 52

S
Sausages · 48

Simple Cheese Sandwich · 15

Simple Lamb Chops · 86

Slum Dunk Brisket · 62

Spatchcock Turkey · 72

Spiced Brisket · 57

Spicy Chicken Breasts · 77

Spicy Chinese Cumin Lamb Skewers · 82

Spinach and Egg Scramble · 12

Steak Marinade · 31

Sticky-sweet Pork Shoulder · 51

Stuffed Grilled Zucchini · 109

Sweet & Tangy Braised Lamb Shank · 92

Sweetheart Steak · 60

Swordfish Steaks with Corn Salsa · 101

T
Tequila Lime Roasted Turkey · 74

Tomato Scrambled Egg · 16

Turkey Breast · 70

Turkey Legs · 76

Turkey Sandwich · 23

W
Wine Flavored Leg of Lamb · 91

Y
Yan's Roasted Quarters · 71

Z
Zucchini with Red Potatoes · 107

Printed in Great Britain
by Amazon